Patricia Cor___ll__ ?l__ are
a very special ___nd.
Courage is a strong _____
and you have it. Let this
be just the beginning for
you and may God shine His
face upon you and be gracious
to you.!!! I love you my
friend.

Love
Jacquelin
Hampton
Beverly

Rise Up

JACQUELINE HAMPTON-BEVERLY

ISBN 978-1-0980-8340-3 (hardcover)
ISBN 978-1-0980-8341-0 (digital)

Christian Faith Publishing, Inc.
832 Park Avenue
Meadville, PA 16335
www.christianfaithpublishing.com

Printed in the United States of America

Book Dedication

My Lord, my Lord, I dedicate my life story to You, Jesus Christ. I have so much to be grateful for, including all the times You saved me from death. Thank you, Lord, for not giving up on me. I love you with all my heart, mind, body, and soul.

Acknowledgement

There have been many people who have been instrumental in my growth as a person. Everyone who touched my life, you know who you are. I have mentioned some of you in my book directly. So I will only mention those right now that had a word from God and delivered it on time so that I would not give up in the process. Steven who prophesy over my life, that came directly by Holy Spirit, and the young lady that told me that God said my prayers was powerful. The man in the car at the traffic light (angel). My spiritual mentor, Kregg Lilly, who has always delivered the messages from God throughout the last five years of my journey. There is one who has been by my side on this spiritual journey, Danise Lilly, who has stuck by me and has not been afraid of the naysayers concerning me. Yvonne and Yvette Taylor, for just being there. Thank you, all. May God bless you more than He has blessed me, in Jesus Christ name. Amen.

"Oh my goodness! What in the world is going on? Look at all these cops riding the block like this!" I said to myself while telling the driver of the car to watch the road. I am watching these cops ride up and down the street, as we are about to pull up to a crack house. I am trying to act calm, as to not show my desperation to run!

There are three of us in the car. Donna, who is the driver—and by the way, she is high as a kite, in other words, she is acting like a cracked-out hoe; Mike, who gave me the money for the dope; and myself. By the way, neither Mike or myself is high yet, and frankly, Donna is being kind of annoying but it's her car and so we got to put up with her crap.

Now me and Donna get out of the car like we got nerves of steel and walk in the crack house anyway. Any sensible person or not-so-hard-up-for-dope person would have just kept driving and went to another crack house, but when you know the dope is good and this is the spot, 'cause your boys are up in here and you know you are going to get your money's worth, then you do what we did, be bold, stupid and go on inside.

Never in a million years was I prepared for how this heifer was going to act coming out of the crack house. This crazy—a—woman is hounding me for my crack, after she had just bought her own. I am telling you, right in front of these cops, this broad is tripping, who by the way are still rolling and watching us. My mistake was letting this crazy, cracked-out broad drive us to the crack house in the first place. Me and Mike should have walked to the dope house because it was close enough to where he lived.

We get into her car and I am warning her to turn around in the seat and drive and keep her eyes on the road. So as we drive off, she is still hounding me for the dope I got, so much so that she can't even drive straight. She is turning around in the seat and everything, looking at my dope, like she must make sure I am not doing anything to it until we get to Mike's house, instead of watching how she is driving. (Straight up crackhead.) I am sitting back here praying that this heifer doesn't get us busted. Does she know the kind of technology that exists today? She is in a zone, and she can't come out of this like spell or even comprehend that she is about to get us busted. So the inevitable happens next. Yep, the siren goes off and we get pulled over. I don't have time to get rid of the dope. I could have put it in her seat but that wouldn't have been the right thing to do, so I didn't do it. I kept it in my pocket and prayed some more. On the outside I seem cool, calm, and collected but on the inside, I am frantic!

The first thing that flashed through my mind was my family and what they would think of me after being clean for seven years, what a disappointment and failure I would be all over again.

The cop gets out of his car and immediately comes to the driver's window and asks us for our IDs. He goes back to his cop car, and I am sitting there thinking, *How am I going to get rid of this dope?* I am so furious at Donna that I can't even think of where to put the dope.

I then ask Donna what the cop is doing, and she says, "He is coming on your side of the car."

Before I could do anything else, the cop snatches my door open and tells me to get out of the car. (It takes longer than that to run your name through the computer but that was evidence that they already knew who I was.) After stepping out of the car, this man cop is shoveling his hands in my pockets. I am getting upset with him and feeling very uncomfortable because my knowledge of this kind of situation is that a woman cop should be doing this. He then pulls out a newly bought crack pipe and says to me, "What is this?"

I wanted to say, "What does it look like, smart guy?" but I had to refrain from getting smart mouthed, because that was definitely not going to help my situation that I am currently facing. So I go to stick my hand in my other pocket, and he stops me, and he sticks his hand in that pocket and pulls out the twenty-dollar rock of crack cocaine. Once he has the dope in his hand, lifting it up, out of nowhere, cop cars start barreling in from down the street and around the corners (a sting operation, I guess). There were too many cop cars. My thought now, we were just the little people in a bigger picture and why are they wasting valuable time and money on three smokers, when in fact two cop cars would have been enough (Drama@queens.com).

They handcuffed me, and they grabbed Donna out of the car and handcuffed her too. She has dropped all her dope on the floor of her car, and although it was all crumbled up, it was still visible. Next, they tell Mike to get out of the car and they searched him as well. When they didn't find anything on him, they let him go. Imagine me with Mike's crack rock in my pocket. Busted again with someone else's dope in my pocket. When was I ever going to learn?

The Beginning

If anyone would have told me that fairytales don't come true, I would have wanted to stay in my mama's stomach. I could see me shouting out to her right now, "I wanna stay in here, Mama, where it is nice and warm and safe, I'm not coming out there, Mama. Send me back."

It was the winter of 1960 when I came kicking and screaming into this world; at least this is how I would have imagined it happened. Mama said that I wasn't waiting for the doctors or the nurses to get prepared. I just popped right out. The hospital where I was born was called Dixie Hospital. In fact, all my sisters were born here.

I am the third child and the middle of the five children that my mom had. Some kids hate being the middle child, but I knew deep inside that there awaited something spectacular for this middle child because of all the emphasis that generations have spoken against the middle one. I have lived to break that curse and to rise up above the gibberish and the misconstrued notion that we are the bad sheep or bad apple of the bunch.

Let me introduce my parents first. My dad, Joseph Hampton was born in Machipongo, Virginia, to Catherine and Joshua. My mom, Barbara, was born in Suffolk, Virginia, to Grace and Henry Clark.

My name is Jacqueline, named after the president's wife Jacqueline Kennedy. Also, my last name is the same as the city I was born in, Hampton, Virginia. A lot of great people started out their lives in this part of the world, and so, why not me.

Anyway, when my dad met my mom, she had a child already and that would be my eldest brother, Rickey, and my dad adopted

Rickey as his own. Then after they got married, Kim my oldest sister was born, then me, Karen Yvette, and Joanne would then come when I was twelve years old.

We lived in a little red house on a street named Pocahontas Place. Probably two bedrooms and not big enough for a growing family such as ours.

The coolest and earliest (three years old) memory about this place was we had a fig tree in the backyard that me and my brother and sister often got in trouble over. We were told many times by our parents to stay off that fig tree, but the figs were so good. They would always know we had been eating them because the stains of the figs would be all over our clothes. Imagine three little children bare-footed, dirty from playing outside making mud pies, eating figs and the mud pies and showing up at the back door crying 'cause Mama just told us we gonna get a whooping from being under that fig tree again. You would think we would have learned from the many times that they told us before, but the figs were so good, though.

If this was someone else's story, they probably would say, "Well, we lived a pretty normal life," but that is not my story. My family life was just as dysfunctional as it could get. I could say, we grew up in church and we did, but not so much with our parents. They would drop us off at Sunday school. Then when Sunday school was over, we would go upstairs to the Sanctuary for Church. Most of the time we would call for them to pick us up or they would give us bus fare to catch the bus home.

My dad was a very hard man. We got beatings if we didn't know what the preacher preached about, and don't let someone say we did something in church 'cause we were going to get a whooping for that too. There was this one time that I remember so well. I was excited to get home and tell my parents about the snake in the tree that made Eve eat the apple.

As for me, I have always wanted to be on top of the world, but it always seemed like the world was sitting on top of me. I have always felt out of place and maybe this was God's plan for me, never fitting in. There has always been something about me, that not even I can put my finger on. I have had some unforgettable moments in my life that I knew were God orchestrated and after looking back over my life and yet no one ever understood or would even believe me when I shared them. I can't let that stop me from believing that God's hand has been on my life from the very beginning.

I started having dreams as a little girl, and I have never really known the meaning of any of them. I have some idea of what they could mean, but I'll wait and ask Jesus when I see Him.

The first one I remember was this: there was this row of hedges separating the front yard from the backyard. Kim and I would jump off the back porch and run and claw our way through these hedges. The branches never seemed to cooperate with me as I would be trying not to get tangled and snagged in the thicket of the overgrown bushes. Once through them we would then run and try to make it to the front porch before this horse would try to get us. I remember being deathly afraid of that horse. Now here is the odd thing about the dream, I dreamt the dream more than once.

Kim would always make it to the front porch, but I would always get caught in the hedges. I would never make it to the front porch before I would wake up out of the dream. I remember very vaguely calling out to my sister to help me because I would always get caught in the bushes, but she would never come back to help me. After about a year, I guess of having the dream, I finally made it to the front porch when I awoke. After that, I never had the dream again. Only now do I have a slight clue of what it means. By and by, it all makes sense as the rest of my destiny unfolds.

Let me tell you that life was just life clawing my way through those hedges. It has been a struggle all my life to achieve and to make it from one thing to the next. I would wake up every day trying not to make the same mistakes over and over again. Sometimes it worked out and other times it was a downhill battle, trying to keep from falling flat on my face. I wanted to make my parents proud of me, but for whatever reason, that never happened.

The one and only time I felt special when I was a kid was when my Aunt Joan, my mom's younger sister, had been living with us for as long as I can remember. She was never not there. My Aunt Joan was Aunt Pony until she announced that she was getting married and then we called her Aunt Joan. So the special part comes in when she is planning her wedding, and I get picked by her to be her flower girl. You talk about special, at five years old, I remember this like it was yesterday. I remember my mom taking her time to do my hair extra pretty, and my clothes were the best. The little laced socks with all the ruffles, the dress was flowing with layers. The patent leather shoes that were shining like new money. They had me looking like a million-dollar baby. When I walked down that aisle, it was the most amazing time ever. I didn't want it to end. I probably would never get this much love and attention ever again. I savored that moment.

We moved when I was four years old into a brand-new house. Nine new houses and nine black families in our new little cul-de-sac. Everybody spoke to one another and us kids were taught to respect other people's properties, especially their yards. It wasn't the perfect little world, but for the most part it was peaceful. I've learned one thing in life, that if it looks good on the outside, you can darn well believe that there is dysfunction on the inside in most cases.

Aside from not needing anything, we had the best of both worlds. When I say this, I mean the good and the bad. We had the best Christmases that any kid could have growing up, and on the same hand, we had a dad who used to beat the crap out of us. One of his favorite sayings was, "I'm gonna let you slide this time." But did that matter? Because as soon as the wind blew, we were in trouble all over again and I am literally talking about before the day ended. It was if he looked for a reason to beat us.

My siblings and I all had something that made us stand out. I, for instance, was the spitting image of my dad. My dad friends would call me "little Hamp." It occurred to me that this still did not have any merit of love with my dad toward me; maybe if I had been a boy then he would have been proud when they said this. He always blew it off, like I was a nobody.

My dad was the heavy one, and my mom was the more of a gentler soul. My mom would play with me and my sisters. She taught us how to play bobby jacks and all kinds of card and board games but no card games on Sundays. It was forbidden.

Mama did give her share of whoopings. She would tell us to go outside and get a switch off the peach tree, and by the way, maybe that's why that peach tree never ever produced any peaches bigger than a cherry.

My dad, on the other hand, did not take any interest in being nice or interacting with us when it came to playing games. Now there were a couple of times as a child that he played softball with us only because the kids on the block would beg him and a couple of the other parents to play with us. It was more for a show than anything else with him.

His laughter or joy came out when he dealt with other people, but not with his children and very little with my mom as well. I loved to see my dad and mom get along, but again, my dad was a bitter man and so it wasn't often that he was the loving husband. I don't know what caused this man to be this way; maybe the military did this or maybe he was deprived of having his dad around when he was growing up.

My dad is the one who disciplined us the most. He never told us he loved us until he gave us these long, drawn-out talks before he would beat us. It went something like this: "This is going to hurt me more than you." Me thinking to myself, *Liar, liar pants on fire. There is no way this whooping was going to hurt you more than me.* As a child, I got more whoopings than I care to remember. I could count the times I didn't get a whooping compared to the times that I did. If we made it a week without one, it was amazing. We would have to wear long pants and long-sleeve blouses to cover up the whelps before going to school, so we would not get made fun of by the other kids. All the kids on our block, though, knew what kind of dad we had, and they all knew we were afraid of him. Even they were intimidated by him.

Back to the beatings, though, depending on what mood he was in determined how long the beating would last. It seemed as if he didn't get tired. I believed his frustration with life came out on us when he was whooping us. We would stand or sit and wait for our turn while we watch the other sibling get their whooping. I remember us kids, laughing and joking later about how the other one would

15

act when getting their whooping. Believe me, it was not funny when we were getting them.

We were not bad kids, but let my dad tell it, we were the worst on the block. He compared us to all the other people's kids all the time. Their grades, their dispositions as kids. Maybe because their parents encouraged them instead of beating them all the time.

We were the only kids that were not allowed to go over the other kid's houses. My dad was so strict, it made us nervous and uncomfortable to be around him.

Whatever was going on with my dad when we were growing up was not in our favor. Maybe it had something to do with how he was raised. Not that my grandmother was a bad person at all. In fact, my grandmother was a good grandma for the most part. She lived with us for a long time or what seemed to be a long time. But it could have been different for him because he was the only boy with two sisters. I don't know, but I do know that he loved his mother or maybe he had too out of respect and the fact that she raised the three of them by herself.

Being a child in the sixties in my family, we did not have conversations concerning the things going on in the world. When busing happened in our city, it was no big deal for us. We just went with the flow. TV news did not interest me either because we were not included in the adult world and I guess that is okay on some levels, but now looking back, I might should have paid more attention to those events. Like, when Martin Luther King got shot when I was seven years old, it didn't mean much to me. The adults seemed to be pressed about it, but to a seven-year-old little girl, life was difficult enough with trying to be good and not get beat to death. It was also around this time when Martin Luther King died that we experienced trouble from the white teenagers that lived behind my dad's field. They started trouble by throwing apples and sending bottles filled with cloth hanging out of them set on fire. The police were called and the fire department on more than one occasion. The police kept telling us that they had to catch them in the act. Guess what the police was never there to catch them in the act. My parents and some other neighbors came together to do a neighborhood watch. I also remember my dad talking to the kid's parents, but they kept denying that their boys were doing anything. Time went by and things got quiet. I believe the parents eventually put a stop to their boys harassing us.

We were always on the tail end of the conversation that the grown folks were having. They would always make us get out away from them when they were talking about grown folk stuff (ear-hustling was what we were trying to do). Nowadays, kids know everything because they are right in the middle of the conversations.

My sisters and I experienced being in a few activities like the Brownies and then on to Girl Scouts, but after a while, my dad stopped us from going to those activities. Just like when I started to learn how to swim, he stopped that too, along with the piano lessons. Later in life, he wondered why I couldn't finish anything that I started, and that's because he had engrained that into me with his inconsistency in allowing us to finish what he started. The only thing consistent about my dad was the whooping's he gave us.

As a child, I do have some good memories. The first concert that I ever went to see was "The Jackson Five." It was phenomenal! Going to this concert was one of the biggest surprises that me and my sisters ever got. It was unbelievable. My dad's entertainment for us was amusement parks, the beach, the rodeo and fishing a couple of times, but never a concert and never without him. The only time we ever took a long trip as a family was to New York for my cousin Loretta's high school graduation and that was because she had spent some years with us, and he was fond of his two sister's children.

Christmas dinner at our house was a feast with leftovers for days. My mom was the chef in our house, and she was good at it. The spread consisted of sweet potato pie, chitlins, turkey, gravy, oyster stuffing, collard greens, green beans, potato salad, ham, gravy, duck, yams, rice, cakes, and cranberry sauce. My grandma would make the world's best homemade rolls to top it off.

This is the one and only time that my dad interacted with us in a good fashion. There was so much laughter and just an awesome time. At Christmas, we saw a side of him that we didn't see often.

Being a kid was short-lived for my siblings and me because my dad decided that he wanted to start up a florist when I was about ten years old. If life hadn't already been bad enough.

It started out as us doing little task to long days in the fields. We worked from sunup to sundown, and to make it even worse, he figured out a way to put a light in the backyard to shine into the field behind our house so we could work past dark. We watered plants (there were no irrigation system), we planted plants, and we pulled weeds. The weeds were never ending. Our hands would be all torn up from the thorns and the tougher weeds. We just sucked up the blood and kept right on plowing through. There was no such thing as an "owie" or bandage to cover it up.

One of the tasks was taking black tar cans off the truck and throwing them on the can pile on the hill. This was the worst thing ever because usually we didn't have enough gloves to go around and someone would always have black hands afterward, due to the cans being freshly dipped in tar. The only way to get the tar off our hands was to first rub our hands in dirt and then pour either gasoline or paint thinner on our hands. I soon learned that the reason why they dipped the cans in tar was to keep the cans from rusting.

We learned every aspect of taking a cutting of a shrub and growing it up to be a big bush or tree. We supplied all the florists in the surrounding area. We even supplied a Sears store in our city. We had little orders and big orders and it required everybody working to get these big tasks done. We worked like slaves. You know, Sunday was supposed to be a day of rest and rest never came.

My dad never hired men to help him. He used us meaning my brother and sisters, his mom, our cousins, and my mom. He even would pay the neighbor money to help at times. Sometimes the kids around our block would help, just so we could come play with them. This became a chore trying to get some play time in.

My brother Rickey worked the fields for two years before they sent him away to my granddaddy because of his mischievous ways. But again, if you were constantly on the hit list of our dad, you would be mischievous too.

Daddy wanted a boy so bad, so when my mom got pregnant when I was twelve years old, Daddy dreamed of having a boy.

On the day that Mama went into labor, my dad took her to the hospital, but it was taking so long, he came home. When she had delivered the baby, my auntie called, and my dad answered the phone. She told him that it was a girl and it was the first time I saw my dad shed a tear. I looked at him and he said in a very low voice, "It's a girl" and walked off. He blamed my mom for not giving him a boy, and after that, their marriage started going down the tube.

He complained that we were not helping him the way we should. That Mama was lazy just like the kids. Things got worse, and this put me and my older sister in jeopardy of treatment undeserving of his wrath.

My dad's full-time job was working as a nursing assistant at the VA hospital. He worked the evening shift and so he went to work at 3:00 p.m., five days a week. This allowed us a time to breathe but it did not eliminate his to-do list, that he would leave our mom so that when we got out of school, straight into the field we would go. My grades suffered and my interest in everything was gone. I tried playing the bass cello in junior high school and the clarinet in high school, but I was never good at either because of the work environment and the pressures of him beating us when we brought bad grades home. He's not realizing or even taking credit for the reason why we were failing. It was hard being a kid.

I remember taking a trip to Niagara Falls with the band when I was in high school at Hampton High School. I almost didn't get to go because my daddy tried to sabotage it, but my mom somehow stepped in and made it happen. When I got back from the trip, he added extra work to my already overwhelming amount of duties.

School for me was a refuge and a hard place. A refuge from the tedious work at home. A hard place because of the bullying that I experienced at school. Let me explain. I had reasonably long hair when I was growing up. It was curly and silky. My mom decided to take me to the beauty shop to get a perm at the age of ten. After that, my hair started to fall out. It got so short that the kids at school started to make fun of me. I eventually started wearing a wig. One day, this girl in junior high school pulled my wig off. I was so embarrassed and hurt because all the other kids started laughing at me.

My sister Kim found out and told me that I was going to fight this girl and she would have my back if anything went down the wrong way. Well, everyone in the school found out that we were going to fight. There was a mob of kids following us after school because we had to take the fight off the school grounds. I am telling you; it was the biggest crowd ever formed for a fight. When we arrived at the designated place, words started and then I knew I had to throw the first punch, and when I did, that was all she wrote. Kim stepped in and beat that girl like she stole something (maybe my wig), *laughing*. After that I didn't have any more trouble out of that girl. My sister was a beast. Kim did not appear to be a fighter but every now and again it would come out. Even the boys at school knew not to mess with me and my younger sister because of Kim. All of this, though, did not eliminate the uncomfortable way I felt about being called ball headed. What I didn't realize back then though is that I was a beautiful little girl despite the short hair, but no one ever told me. Maybe because I didn't share my feelings with anyone due to the shame I felt 'cause of not having long hair anymore. Me and my older sister were being taught to be strong and don't be wimps. Maybe that was our saving grace for what would come later in life.

My dad treated us like boys instead of girls. He once told us that he was training us up to be independent and to not have to count on a man to take care of us when we got older. Kim and I were stronger than all the boys our age, physically and mentally. I distinctly remember my dad bringing a white birch tree home one day and told Kim and me to take that tree off the back of the truck and put it on the hill. Now, the ball of dirt on this tree was five times bigger than either one of us and we could not get our arms around it. How we picked that tree up that day should have been recorded. Thank God, we didn't throw our backs out.

One day, I believe I was thirteen years old, and I was working in the field alone because my dad had opened a flower shop, Hampton's Flower Garden, to do some retail selling. Now we have gone from wholesaling to retail sells. My mom ran it and my oldest sister got to go with her more than me. My dad used to say that I was the lazy one and so I had to stay and work in the field. This man seemed as if he hated me. What he didn't know is that I had a strong desire not to be a fulltime worker in his part time business. I hated it with a passion. So much so that I prayed a lot. I often wanted to run away but I didn't know where to run to.

So on this one day while being in the field all alone. It was hot and I was tired and hungry, but I knew that I had to stay at it, because I never knew when my dad would show up. I am out there pulling weeds behind the can pile.

Now, as a child, this field looked very big in size. It had about ten rows, five feet across and fifty feet long on one side. Then the other side of the field was about fifteen rows, five feet across and sixty feet long. Then there were a few short rows behind the black can pile, which the cans were used to plant the plants in.

I was pulling weeds behind the black can pile on one of the shorter rows. I was on my knees crying little tears because I was tired. So I began to pray: "Dear God, if you are the Son of God, Jesus, please make it rain because I am tired, and I want to go in and rest and make me a sandwich."

What you got to see here is that there were no clouds in the sky when I began to pray. All of a sudden, the clouds began to roll in, and within minutes, it began to rain. Drops at first and then pouring down came the rain. I started crying tears of joy. I ran into the house and called my Aunt Joan and told her what had just happened. I don't know if she believed me or not, but it happened and from that day forward I believed that Jesus was real, and He had heard my prayer. This was the greatest day of my life as a child. (Later on, in life, I discovered that God had made it rain because of the prayers of Elijah in the Bible.) This did my heart good.

Most of you are wondering at this point in my story, where is her mom? My mom for the most part had "no say" if my dad "said first." She did not override him and if she did then a big argument would ensue, and she did her best to stay away from those types of confrontations. Our life was always feeling out his mood, because if he wasn't happy, no one was going to be happy. I remember one time my mom had packed her suitcase and was going to leave us with this man, we called Dad, but after much pleading she stayed. This was the first time that I knew of him putting his hands on her. It was not easy, living in this environment and I didn't understand how my mom continued to keep us and her in this upside-down situation. I smiled anyway as a child. No one knew that I hated my life. I just kept going because I knew I had too. I prayed even more after that day in the field, realizing that God hears prayers. I prayed that he would get my mom, my sisters and I, out of this horrible life. A child should never have to live in fear their entire childhood. Fear of a parent, scared to move, smile, laugh, or do anything that would set him off. By the way, my dad didn't cuss, drink alcohol, or smoke cigarettes ever. He was just that strict.

In one night, everything changed. We were lying in our beds, and we heard my mom and dad arguing over something, maybe his infidelity. Anyway, it went from arguing to him beating her. We could hear her crying out. The same tears she was crying, we were too. My oldest sister Kim shows up at my bedroom door and she is screaming at me in almost a loud whisper to come on. I am looking at her like "What are we going to do?!" So she grabbed me, and as she was pulling me down the hallway, we passed the kitchen door and I could see him and her down on the steps in the den with her between his legs, him beating her with his belt, like she was his child. All I can hear her saying as she is crying "Stop, Hamp."

My mind is racing, my heart is pounding. I am feeling scared and thinking what gives him the right to beat my mom like that. What makes a man beat on a woman that he claims that he loves? "If you don't love me then leave me, but don't beat me in the mist of your own pain, anger, and bitterness as if I was the cause of your unhappiness."

We ran out the front door and across the street to the neighbor's house to call my mom's sister. My Aunt Joan must have broken every rule of the road to get to us. When she gets there, Kim and I go and meet her, getting out of her car. The three of us walk back into the house. By now, my dad has stop beating my mom. I can see my mom coming down the hallway with her face red and tears streaming down. As my mom made her way toward us, my dad is now in a full-blown argument with my aunt and he has no intentions on leaving the house. Now truth be told, I believe my dad knew my Aunt Joan was no joke when it came to standing up to a man because my Aunt had in the past stood up to her older brother, Uncle Rabbit, and my dad knew of this incident because it had taken place in our house years before. So with that, my dad was in a stand down mode that we had never seen before. My Aunt Joan tells us to grab my baby sister and tells my mom to come on. My Aunt Joan is acting like she has a gun in her purse by holding her purse a certain kind of way but later we learn that it was just a ploy to get us out of the house.

My mom's brothers and her dad were not going to be as kind as my Aunt Joan. But by the time they found out and came the next day, my dad had hightailed it to his hometown, the Eastern Shores.

After that night, my mom lost a lot of weight and things were never the same again. She was scared to be around my dad, and she stayed with her sisters and sent us back home. I was just hoping that my mom would not bail out on us. The two younger sisters didn't have that to worry about but me and Kim is about to finish up our first year of high school and leaving us might have been a thought.

My dad acted like a different man after this. It was as if he was disappointed with life and with us. Were we supposed to sit back and let him abuse our mom both physically and mentally as he had done to us? No! The travesty is that we never got to really know the other side of my dad. We got glimpses of his good nature, but it was short-lived. He was better to other people then he was to his wife and children. It was as we were strangers.

My dad eventually told my mom that he would not be putting his hands on her again. So she came back home too. We didn't stay long after that. My mom's oldest brother, Uncle June, came to Virginia and flew my mom and my two youngest sisters back to Arizona with him and his family. The following week, I flew by myself to Arizona. I was about thirty-two years old before I ever saw my daddy again.

Let me say this: as little girls, we did not have a loving relationship with our dad. We were not daddy's little girls.

All my prayers were "God, please get us away from this man." God heard me. Amen.

Note to self: Always pray.

Growing Up

The summer of 1976 is when I moved to Tucson, Arizona. I boarded a plane by myself for the first time ever and I felt confident enough to know that I could do this. I was fifteen years old, with all kinds of thoughts running through my mind. First, "God, please don't let this plane fall out the sky and please get me to Tucson in one piece."

Then, what would living in the desert be like and would I immediately connect with my cousins? My mind was racing so much and the excitement of it all, I didn't even consider that I was traveling alone, at fifteen, and vulnerable. I had a layover in Chicago, Ohara, airport, considered then to be the biggest airport in the US, so my uncle said. When I was walking through the airport to get to the next gate, it was if someone was with me. Maybe an angel. I say that because I remember so well that, I just started walking and walked right to the gate. I didn't feel the least bit scared. I boarded the plane and tried to sleep, so I wouldn't have to think about the plane being in the sky. The best part of the plane ride was the takeoff and the landing, I loved it.

The plane finally stopped and as I look out the window, I notice that we have not pulled all the way up to the building of the airport but stopped out away from it. Everyone on the plane started jumping to their feet immediately as the seat belt light goes off. So I do what they do, but a little hesitant because thoughts are flooding my brain. I gather my things and my thoughts, looking back to make sure that I haven't left anything on the seat and trying not to get in nobody's way. Moving down the aisle, toward the door of the plane, the thoughts that don't matter anymore are gone, replaced by a grateful heart. Grateful to God, for what He has done. My own silent prayer in my mind, "Thank you, Jesus, for answering my prayers." Now, I am thinking about the life I just left and the life I am about to step into.

Before my foot came down on the first step outside the plane, the hot blistering heat and wind hit my whole body at the same time. "What is this? Is someone playing a trick on me!" I panic, not understanding or comprehending what I am feeling. That desert air hit me in the face, and I wanted to cry. It was hot. I thought I had just stepped into a furnace like the Hebrew boys. How was I going to survive this? You know that saying "Out of the frying pan into the fire"? This was me. "Focus, Jackie," that is what I had to tell myself so I wouldn't lose it in front of all these people. My uncle had talked about this place like this was the place to be. I wanted to call him a straight-up liar, but as a kid still, I had to mind my manners. I wanted to turn around and go back to Virginia. But no one would be there for me, and so I stumbled down the steps only to remember what was behind me. Surely there would be air-conditioning when I got to my uncle's house.

As I entered the building, I laid eyes on my uncle, with his teddy bear-looking self. My Uncle June was a big man, and there is no way I would miss him. I was so glad to see him and the smile that he gave me made me forget about the furnace that I just stepped out of only for a minute. Me, being a kid, begin to complain about the heat. He said, "This is the desert, girl, get used to it."

My Uncle June worked at the Tucson International Airport. My plane had got in just in time for him to get off work.

The complaining continued all the way to his house due to the car being old and no air-conditioning.

As we are making our way to the house, I am so excited about seeing the cactus. I probably asked my uncle a hundred questions before we even got to the house, especially about the rattlesnakes and scorpions, that I thought were hanging out all over the place, but that was not the case. The desert was fascinating to me. My eyes probably were as big as the smile that was on my face as I looked out of the window of the car as we made our way to the house. Words cannot explain the joy and peace that I felt starting a whole new life. I wanted to pinch myself to make sure it was all real.

Yes, this place was going to take some getting used to.

My Uncle June loved to laugh, and he talked with me a lot. I liked my uncle. He was the kind of uncle who knew everything and even if he didn't, he would make it up as he went. We used to call people like this a walking encyclopedia, but I would call it Mr. Know-It-All. It was all in fun, though, 'cause the stories that he would tell us was hilarious even though half of them was made up or hard to believe.

When he would go to get in his car, I would try to find out where he was going so that I could go with him. I loved my Uncle June and he loved us back.

Remember I said my mom had a gentler spirit. Well, it was so. She was allowing us some freedom that we did not have back home. Before, in Virginia, the only one of us that could visit friend's houses was my younger sister Ebie (Karen Yvette), but now we all have the liberty to venture out.

Right across the street, there is a park outside my uncle's front door, and we are now living in an area where black people are hanging out all over the place (south park). Who would have guessed in the desert? My thought was cowboys and Indians but never black people in the middle of the desert.

History, a lot of times don't tell the whole truth. People who are writing the story, omit the things that some of us would have loved to have known, especially telling us that there were black cowboys. None of my textbooks ever told me that the wild, wild west had black people in it (laughing).

My uncle has five kids of his own and we are all living in his four-bedroom house. The oldest is Johnny, who was twenty years old. Then Milton, who was closer to my age. Jana, Lily, and Mark the baby boy who was about seven years old. My Aunt Sarah, I had never known or met 'cause my uncle had lived out here in the west, had died a couple of years before we came.

My mom and I take my uncle's room. My sisters sleep in the room with our girl cousins and my uncle now sleeps on the couch. It was interesting, but better than sleeping under the same roof with a dad who showed us no love.

I moved to Tucson about a month before school started. I would be going to the eleventh grade. I am getting excited to start school and find out if it was going to be any different from going to school in Virginia. Hopefully the bullying would not occur, like I had experienced before.

I wish I could remember the first day of school at Tucson High, but the memory is gone. I do know that; it was not like Hampton High at all. Hampton High was all one building and Tucson High had four buildings. There was the main building that was approximately eighty years old. The gym, cafeteria and Auto mechanics building, but I am sure they called that building something else. The school provided more independence than what I was used to. I came from a very controlled environment in Virginia, and Tucson provided so much freedom and room to get used to. It was like being in a candy and toy store all at the same time. Nobody was watching me like a hawk but on the flip side of that, knowing in the back of my mind that I must do the right thing even though no one was watching me. There was no one to influence me at first. So the disciplines that I had been raised with, kept me in check.

Trying to find my way in this ginormous school and having to get from one class to the other in the allotted time was not going to be easy. It was an art to get to my locker and then to the next class before that second bell rang. It took planning of how many books you had to take and what material you needed for which classes was in that building and if I would have enough time to come back to my locker before going to the next building for gym or whatever else I had to do to make it all work. I eventually came up with a plan with one of my friends so that she and I had access to two lockers in different buildings, to accomplish being on time. It worked out great.

Then came the even tougher part of high school was getting around the right crowd. The great thing about me, I wanted to belong, but I had to pick and choose my friends carefully due to bad experiences in elementary and junior high school. I know I shared just a little bit earlier in my story about the whole short hair ordeal.

Nothing had changed from this time to that, they still made fun of me. I endured and tried not to let it affect me.

I joined the band and that is where I met my first friend, Sherry. Then she introduced me to her friends. It was a total of seven girls. They were all in the tenth grade. One in particular, didn't like me but I was okay with that because she was not always around as much.

Anyway, the eleventh grade was a blast. We did the usual things like ditching class to go downtown and hang out which was in walking distance. This was truly a life change for me because I had never had a group of friends, that their parents gave them so much freedom. Interesting thing about this is that my oldest sister Kim, had her friends and I had mine. We were now living in two very different worlds. My sister's friends were two twin sisters and their lifestyle was more in the poorer neighborhood. Although the neighborhood, we lived in, wasn't much better, but my friend's parents were in the nicer neighborhoods. It may seem irrelevant now but down the road it plays a part in my story.

In this group of girls, though, I was a tom girl, and I liked sports and they were all on the cheerleader side of the spectrum. I went out for the tennis team. I was awesome at serving the ball, but my stamina was not good. My time on the tennis team was short-lived. I still loved the game and would often hit balls off this wall to get exercise and stay fit.

More toward the end of the school year Sherry and Bonnie introduced me to house parties, where I felt very out of place. I could not dance and that was an embarrassing time in my life. Bonnie and her sisters showed me how to get by, so that it would be less of an awkward time for me. I hung out with Bonnie a lot more and got to become close to her family. It was special 'cause Bonnie was the type of person who, take you like you come, and I loved that about her.

One weekend in May of 1977, I stayed over Sherry's house. We had gotten up early Saturday morning. She had chores to do, so I was helping her out. I was in her room, when I heard her yelling at someone out the back door. My curiosity had me rushing into the kitchen to see who she was talking too. It was her neighbor across the alley. He yells to tell her to come over and she tells me to come along.

I am a little reluctant because this guy looks to old from a distance and not very appealing. Why did my mind go there? I don't know. What difference would that make when all we were going to do is say "hi" and shoot the breeze for a moment. I did not want to go but winded up going anyway, when she explained that he and his family were friends. As we are walking through the back gate, I can see a trailer sitting in the backyard. Moving around the front of the trailer, the door is open, and this man is lying on the bed inside the trailer with a blanket thrown across his midsection not to expose his private parts. I am totally turned off by his lack of discretion. He knew we were coming over; he could have put on a shirt and shorts. Sherry introduced us.

"Jackie this is Robert, Robert this is Jackie." I was not prepared for what fell out of this joker's mouth. He looks at me up and down and he says, "Look at that butter."

I look at Sherry like "What the?" She looks at me and I look at her and she is like eyeing me not to respond to this critter. Then he is like explaining about how fine I was and asking me where did I come from? I don't even remember what I said but I turn and walk away back over to Sherry's house. Sherry shows up at the back door. Grinning and asking me what I thought of him and I said, "Nothing."

She said, "He wants to drive you home." I clearly remember saying, "Absolutely not." She then asks me how are you going to get home and I tell her; I'll figure it out. I hadn't ridden my bike, so that was not an option. Next thing I know, Robert is knocking on the back-screen door, letting himself in. He is grinning and asking me if I want a ride home. I am like, "I don't know you." He looks at Sherry to tell her to tell me that he is cool. After much push back, I finally give in and he runs out the back door, over to his house to get his car. Suddenly, I hear this loud music and it is Robert pulling up in this gray low-rider car. I am like second-guessing myself about going with him. Sherry had given me a little background and told me that he was nineteen years old and that he had a job and lived with his mom, dad, and brothers. She even explained that Vernon who was in our band class, was his brother. I am thinking to myself that this might be all right. So I go and on the way home, I am feeling very shy and don't know what to say. Believe me, he has all the words. Our conversation went something like, "I would like to get to know you." I give him direction to get me home and then as we are pulling up in front of my uncle's house, he asks me for my phone number. I give it to him. Then I get out of the car. Wondering, what in the world just happen.

In the coming weeks we did talk, and he wanted to take me out to a house party and then off into the desert to make out.

I was impressed by Robert and things he had accomplished at the age of nineteen. Me, not realizing that it was all just material. Besides having one of the baddest low-rider's car in Tucson, he also had a brand-new Ford pickup. To a sixteen-year-old young girl, this was impressive. Plus, he had a job at a grocery chain that paid good money and benefits.

I should have cared more about the way he was treating me. The mentality was, if you are just dating, you can still be fooling around with others and I was not for that. I caught him more than once flirting with other girls and there was this one in particularly that I didn't like, and she did not like me either and we were both trying to be in his space at the same time. I am not even going to mention her name. She was what some would call "loose."

It amazes me how a person can go from one dysfunctional relationship to another. This was certainly me. From my dad to now my guy friend. We did not connect as boyfriend and girlfriend. In other words, we were never officially boyfriend girlfriend because I allowed him to take advantage of me because I was in need of attention and he gave it and I accepted with no terms and conditions. I jumped when he called, instead of saying "no." So he used me and probably joked about it with his friends. His friends tried flirting with me to see if I was a loose girl, but I was not in the least bit interested. I was then recognized as "she does not want nobody but him." I was okay with that.

The school year has now come to an end. Robert and his family usually go on vacation every June. Well, Robert had to work, so he could not go. While his family was gone, he invited me over for a weekend. I accepted. I did not feel comfortable in his parent's house while they were on vacation. So after one night, he took me home.

I remember staying over at Bonnie's house and calling my mom one morning to tell her that I was not feeling good, and she asked me if I was pregnant. I said "yes," and she tells me to come home. She asked me when I got home, "What am I going to do about this?"

I called Rob and told him that I was pregnant, and his first words were "I told you I don't want any kids." My thought was "You should have covered it up then." I went on to tell him that it's too late to be thinking like that. So then he says, "So are you going to get an abortion?" I say that I have not decided yet. He tries to strong arm me in telling me that I better go get an abortion because he isn't taking care of no kid.

At this point, I am not sure and the thought of not knowing my baby was terrifying to me. I made an appointment to go to the doctor with the intention of getting the abortion, but still not sure that I would have the nerve to go through with it. My mom is watching my every move and facial expressions. A mother certainly knows her child because after sitting in the waiting room and being called to the back, my mom sensed that I did not want to go through with this abortion and told me to put my clothes on and let's go. We passed the doctor on the way out and scheduled another appointment for my prenatal care. No abortion today. Yay!

The next few months went by without much drama or excitement because when I told Rob that I had decided to keep the baby, he was furious. I didn't care though because this was my decision and I am the one who had to go through it. Rob chose to stop talking to me. I had grown accustomed to survival and this case was no different.

Note to self: When people walk away, let them.

I didn't experience any morning sickness and every day was pretty normal. I would ride my bike over to Bonnie's house. I stayed over there more than I stayed at home. Bonnie had a boyfriend. So our time hanging out was limited but she had a house full of family and I was close to them all.

Summer is just about over and now to go back to school to face all the kids and their stares and talking about me getting pregnant over the summer.

I am now a senior in high school, pregnant, and Rob wants nothing to do with me or the baby. It isn't till late October before I see Rob again. I'm still in love with this man because he showed me attention at first that I had never gotten before. It may not be love, but it was something to want him to be around even after he treated me badly.

When he did come around, I went out with him just because I thought things would change and he would change his mind about the baby (it was only a booty call).

My mom had reservation concerning him, but her kind spirited heart wouldn't allow her to say anything bad about him, even if she did have some negative feelings. The only thing she ever asked me, "Is he going to take care of the baby?"

I said "yes" in hopes that he would. I was hoping fatherhood would kick in the moment the baby came. It's funny now, but it was not funny then, when I used to go looking out the window hoping that he would stop by. Calling him on a regular basis and his mom telling me that he didn't want to talk to me. Leaving messages and having his little brothers say that he is not home. Him promising that he would come by and never showing up. After a while, I stop calling and did my best to focus and get prepared for my last year in high school.

School started and because I was a senior, they couldn't force me to go to the school (Roskruge) where they sent pregnant girls. I was at Tucson High every day until I had the baby. I named him Anthony LeVar. He was a cute baby, light-skinned and looking like my mom. (Rob and I are dark-skinned.) So everybody else tried to deny that it was Rob's, but his mom knew. Rob was not able to be there for the birth, but he tried.

A week after Anthony was born, Rob's mom suggested that I get the baby dedicated and so I took him to Church and dedicated him to the Lord. It was good. Now it is time to get back to figuring out school, while raising my son. Him being born in March, required me to be out for a month and so I missed getting my homework done to graduate. I had to finish high school the following year because I didn't have enough credits. I had to make sure I finished because of the negative comment my dad said to me. See, when I was about three months pregnant, I called my dad and told him. He said to me, "What about school?" and I told him that I would finish. He then said to me, "You will never finish anything." So we will see. I was going to show him. That was my driving force. I graduated Tucson High School, class of '79.

Let's pause and go back to the summer of 1978 when I was supposed to graduate. My mom had met a man in the late part of 1977, and they married in February of 1978. They moved to Denver, Colorado, with my two younger sisters. I am now alone with a baby with nowhere to go and my housing had not been approved yet. I slept in my car for two nights (thank God this was Arizona) before Rob's aunt and uncle offered me a place to stay at their house until my housing came through. After living with Aunt Anna and Uncle Bill for about two months, my housing came through. Now, all of a sudden, Rob wanted to be with me and raise our son.

It was interesting starting out. We worked in the cotton fields, weeding the cotton. I was always concerned about the rattlesnakes but thank God, I never encountered one. Other people, out in the fields talked about seeing them but no one ever got close enough to get bit. The thought of it was pretty scary. As a matter of fact, I have never encountered a rattlesnake in all the time that I lived in Arizona.

Rob and I were inseparable. We did everything together. We cooked, cleaned, and took care of the baby equally. His mom was a great help to us. She babysat for us while we did these odd jobs.

Fishing was on our to-do list, on a regular basis. Every fishing hole in Arizona is where we loved to be. As a matter of fact, Rob's family was big on fishing and camping trips.

It was not until I turned eighteen years old before the influence of marijuana got the best of me, along with cigarettes. Rob had quite a few friends who would come over and hang out and drink forties and smoke weed. I tried it and it was a way of being connected to him and his friends, so I did it. I began trying everything that was offered to me. Black beauties, mushrooms, acid, angel dust, and alcohol. The alcohol though was not something I enjoyed because I could never stand the taste or the feeling of being sick if I drank too much. So soda pop is what I stuck too. Aunt Anna though was not a happy camper when she found out that I had started smoking pot. She told me that it would lead to stronger drugs. I always told her, "No it won't." This is one of those times I should have listened to the adult, but I thought, what does she know? she has never smoked pot in her life.

Note to self: Listen carefully when wisdom is being imparted.

Rob and I for the most part got along good I guess because I didn't have a gauge. I didn't have another relationship to compare it to except that it was better than what I had seen from my dad in some cases.

(Note to dads: Your little girls are watching you and your sons are too.)

Rob was a firm believer that a woman needed to work too. He did not get that from his dad though. His dad took care of his mother. I didn't mind though because work had not been a stranger to me in my life. I was somewhat independent in my thinking, being raised to work hard. I needed my own money.

My first real job was working at a nursing home cleaning. I worked on one of the newer wards and I made sure everything was cleaned to the expectations of the head nurse. So when a job came open at the nursing home for a Physical Therapy Aide, the head nurse recommended me, and I got the job.

This was a career job, but it was not something I enjoyed doing. I can say that I did help an old man walk again. His name was Mr. Briggs and to see the smile on his face was all I needed to feel like I had accomplished something. People often do a job just because of benefits and this one certainly had all the benefits, but it was not for me. I stayed four months and quit. I then got a job at a convenient store. That's when I purchased my second car. Rob worked for the City of Tucson and on the side, we started selling a lot of weed. I was saving money and life was going good. It was a little scary at times, thinking the cops would bust us but for the most part, we would go on weekend trips to cut down on the traffic.

By the time, I was turning twenty-one; Rob wanted to try out for the Seattle Seahawks. Training camp was in Spokane, Washington so we moved to Spokane to live with his cousin Gail. Now the other deciding factor to prompt us to move was we were selling so much marijuana that this was the thing to do before we landed in jail.

Rob tried out for the Seahawks but didn't make it and we winded up staying in Spokane for two years. I never found a job in Spokane and so I watched our Son while Rob worked at being a supervisor for a janitorial company.

At twenty-two years old, I met a young lady named Rachel, at the plasma center, where we donated at. We became friends with her and her family. We had fish fries and often came together to play cards or just hang out.

One day, Rachel needed a ride to meet a friend at a hotel. I drove her because she did not drive. I had stopped her at some stores along the way not knowing what she was purchasing. When we got to the hotel, she invited me to go up with her.

She started pulling things out of the bags and then this white powder like substance. I asked her, "What are you doing?" She answered in almost a whisper, "Just watch." As I look on with curious eyes, she put some water in a glass tube and then some of the white powder, that I suspected to be cocaine. Then she had this little mini torch that she fired up and started heating the glass up. This is unlike what Rob and his friends were doing one time back in Tucson, so I kept watching with wide eyes. She then explained that she was rocking cocaine.

Only one other time did I encounter this free-basing technique, back in Arizona and I threw everybody out of my house because they were using ether and not water and baking soda. I did not want them to burn down my house and I didn't want to land in jail because of their need to try something that they barely knew anything about it (experimenting).

I tried it with Rachel that day, but it was not enough to get addicted too while living in Spokane but enough to spark my curiosity when moving back to Tucson. This is one of those scenes that I wanted to shy away from, so I left, not knowing what she was about to get into with this friend of hers, that was flying in from Seattle. One other time before moving back to Tucson. Our next-door neighbor had asked me over. Not knowing why, maybe to smoke some good marijuana, I suspected but when I stepped in the living room, I could see that she had a plate full of cocaine. She nor I knew what we were doing and wind up pouring like two hundred dollars of it down the drain because we could not get it to rock like Rachel had.

In June of 1983, Rob lost his job and we moved back to Tucson.

After moving back to Tucson, we stayed in Rob's parents' trailer home that was now parked in the front yard and a newer trailer. We tried selling weed again but it did not amount to anything. All our contacts were little to none. His mom even knew what we had been into before we moved to Spokane and she made it clear that we were not too sale marijuana out of her trailer.

Life was different now and the prominence that we had before being known for having the best weed around had all changed. We both had to get jobs. I get a job with the same convenient store company but at a different location. Rob got a job at Hughes Aircraft as a janitor.

Not long after we both started working, we got introduce to Ready Rock (cocaine already rocked). This was not good. Every payday was always the same. Nickel and dime his mom for letting us stay in her trailer and the rest would go on what became Crack. This stuff was so addicting.

We overstayed our welcome in his mom's trailer. To Rob, he seemed as if he didn't care that we were not welcomed anymore. He had this mentality that "these are my parents and they have a responsibility to house me." Wrong answer.

Some of our old friends were becoming addicts because of this so called "crack" and their lives were proof of it, and we were well on our way to becoming addicts too.

One very close friend of ours, had a very good job in a hospital as a specialist in the operating room and the crack got the best of her and her husband. Their abuse of it led to a divorce and both, are dead now. One from an overdose in a Pastor's house and the other one from a man stabbing her to death and he tried to kill her mom too but that was the saving grace because the mom lived to tell, and he is now spending life in prison. RIP Nina and Corell.

We had been back in Tucson for almost a year when I found out I was pregnant. I had told Rob that if we had a second child, we would have to get married. I reminded him of that conversation and so he decided to marry me. I never envisioned having a house wedding, but I guess when you don't have money then you do what is cost affective. Looking back on my life now, I am going to try not to have any regrets. I missed my prom too.

Our second son was born in April of 1984 and his daddy named him Caster and I gave him a middle name of LaQuinn. For the life of me, I don't know why and how he came up with the name "Caster." So just in case my son, when he grew up, didn't like his name, he would be able to use his middle name. I also had to pray over my Son because of my addiction, that he would come out drug-free. I believe he did. He is smart as a whip today and strong as an ox. Thank you, Jesus.

My mother-in-law has now put emphasis on us moving out of her trailer because of our second child. So a couple of months later we moved out. Life was pretty routine and not very exciting because living paycheck to paycheck and no hopes of anything changing was not fun. Going to work, coming home, taking care of my two sons and watching some TV while smoking a joint. Then off to bed to wake up another day to the same thing. There was nothing exciting or no motivation to do anything different. Mainly because I forgot to live. I was too busy trying to live in my husband's world, that I didn't create one for myself. I had no friends and no outlets. My mother-in-law would sometimes invite me to go to bingo.

(Note to self: Live life to the fullest and make every day count).

Now, payday was a different situation all together. Pay some bills and smoke the rest up in either crack or weed. Broke the next day, hung over and tweaking because there are no more drugs and trying to come up with how to get more. Depressing as it was, this was my life.

Crack friends would come by, because it was a place to get high and most of them didn't know where to get the crack from, so that put me in the mix, all the time, because I knew enough of the dope houses to purchase it from and even if I couldn't find a dope house open, there would always be someone hanging around the vicinity of South Park that knew who had it or where I could get it from. (the lifestyle had a particular look).

I didn't think about what effect this was having on my marriage and my children. Although he was doing it right beside me, it was still having a silent affect. We hung in there together because the dysfunctional life, I guess was comfortable. I believe that Rob felt a sense of obligation because he is the one who introduce me to drugs. Just for the record, I had a choice, but sometimes influence is greater than a choice.

(Note to you: Who or what is influencing you).

We were not planning the third child, but she came along anyway. We had a girl despite my husband's mom saying, that the dad side of the family don't have girls. As a matter of fact, three out of her four sons, had one girl each. To top that off me and my sisters have one daughter each. Anyway, I named our daughter Tranise. I had picked her name out long before I ever had any kids. I played around with the thought when I was dating Rob., if we ever had a girl, I would take half his middle name (Tracy) and half of my middle name (Denise) thereby giving her the name Tranise.

During these times of having kids I never stopped working and maternity leave for me was short. A week and I was back at work. Mainly because we could not afford for one us to be without a job. Minimum wage jobs were not cutting it, especially with the drug habits. We lived off the bare minimum, such as three chickens, a roll of hamburger, a bag of potatoes, a couple of boxes of macaroni and cheese, hamburger helper and a few cans of vegetables a week. We had enough toilet paper and enough hygiene to make it weekly. Pampers and baby milk consumed a lot of our money as well, and all of it had to be purchased before we went on our crack binges.

Rob's mom and dad helped us a lot, as well as his Aunt Anna because of our drug addictions. I know his mom prayed for us often.

His mom and aunt were church going women. My prayers for myself were few and far between but when things got really rough, I prayed.

A year had passed since I had my daughter. I find out that I am pregnant again. So the addiction was getting so far out of hand, that I had to get away and so Rob and I decided that I should move to Denver with my sister, Ebie and her family until I had the baby. I am remembering that our marriage was very shaky because the drugs was taking a toll on our life.

Rob thought that with me gone, he could save some money and get prepared for this next child as well as me staying clean through this pregnancy. He moved back in with his mom and I took Caster and Tranise with me to Denver. I was drug free for the rest of my pregnancy. On December 5, Ivory Denise was born. Then Rob came to Denver and took us back to Tucson. So now we have the perfect little family. Two boys and two girls. Shortly after moving back to Tucson the crack habit started up again. It was bad because we had four children and living with Rob's parents again.

I found a job working for an apartment complex, cleaning apartments. It was payday, and all morning long I had contemplated on going to get me some crack on lunchbreak and I did. I went back to work and hid out in vacant apartments getting high and when it was gone, I went again to buy some more after work. I was paranoid wondering if someone would see my bugged-out eyes and know that I was high. The whole time I am getting high I am thinking, *What am I going to tell Rob?* As it got later and later, I didn't know what to do. Rob couldn't come look for me because I had the car and I don't know that he wanted to alert his mom, to use her car to come look for me, since he knew I was getting high. When I get home at 1:00 a.m. in the morning, Rob had nothing to say to me accept, "I want a divorce." At that moment, I knew I had screwed up for real. That was a horrible feeling and I couldn't change that day or make it go away. All I thought to do was to talk to God and ask Him to fix what I had messed up. I got on my knees and ask God not to take my marriage. I had broken my own heart this night, because I felt his was breaking. I laid down and three hours later my eyes opened. There was a cool still feeling in the room. I was thinking to myself;

my baby didn't wake up for her bottle and so I turn over to Rob and I say, "Baby didn't wake up for her bottle." Immediately he looks over at Ivory who is sleeping at the head of our bed on the loveseat. He gets up and he says she's not breathing. I am terrified and screaming at the same time. Everybody in the house is waking up and running toward us. We all are in disbelief, and everybody is crying. We call 911. They send an ambulance and the police comes.

They ask us stupid questions as if we did something to our baby. Come to find out later, she died of SIDS, sudden infant death syndrome. I was left to grieve only for a short time because I had three other children who I had to comfort and care for through this process. The only one who really understood was my oldest son and he was okay, I think. Contemplating on all of this I realized that you have to be careful what you pray for, 'cause your answer may come like you don't expect. God comforted me in ways I can't even explain. I felt He (God) was doing what was best for me. (Addiction isn't no joke.) Rob changed his mind about the divorce, and we decided to move away from Tucson and go to Denver. Nine years in Tucson was enough for me and a brand-new start is what I needed.

(Note to the married addicts: Don't wait on a tragedy to come to destroy your marriage and family). RISE UP!

New Beginning

New place, new start (1988), and I thought a new mind-set would be the ultimate beginning of a new life. It started out great. We stayed with my younger sister, Ebie and her family for a couple of months maybe one and then we found us a house to rent. Life was starting out pretty good in Denver. We moved to a neighborhood called Montbello, where my mom and her husband lived. We got jobs at Samsonite, which we believed we would retire from. We sought out a weed man to get our marijuana from and again life took on that routine living again. Never thinking or contemplating on a more meaningful life.

Note to self: routine doesn't have a voice.

I believe if we could have given up the weed, we might not have looked for the crack or being exposed to people who did it. I don't even remember how it got introduced back into our lives in Denver, but it did.

Drugs was not my friend. Weed made me sluggish, sleepy and hungry and crack made me stupid and chasing it relentlessly. I didn't want to eat, and I lost weight on it. I did not choose it, it chose me. My addiction was fueled by rejection. My husband was not concerned about my happiness or what made me happy. He never asked me once in the entire time we were married, what do you need or what do you desire? As long as he had his beer and his joint, he was good. Maybe a concert every now and again and he was cool. Fishing was also high on his list which became a part of my list. It was his friends that I was associated with. I had none of my own. My greatest downfall was me. I didn't seek to find me, so that I could find the meaning of life or my purpose.

Note to women: Make sure your needs are getting met if his is.

Two things in my life had a hold on me and they were—wanting to be loved and crack. Love was going to have to wait and crack had to go, but how was the question.

I had good character strengths, but they seemed to be misapplied. I did realize that I was a leader and not a follower but people pleasing was my downfall. I just wanted to be loved. If ever the cliché "looking for love in all the wrong places," this was me. I should have looked for love in God, but I didn't know enough about Him. Later on, in this journey, I would find out that just calling on Him when you are in trouble is not truly knowing Him. A relationship is so much deeper.

So as I was saying, back to the same routine in Denver. We went to work, came home, cooked dinner, rolled a joint and watched TV for the rest of the evening until bedtime. Drug friends came by on occasion to smoke weed and then someone mention crack and everything inside of me stands at attention for the desire, all over again. This is what is interesting to me; it was never friends of mine that brought the drugs, because for one, I didn't have any friends. Remember I said I lived in his world. It's hard to see the dysfunction in your life when you are right smack dead center of the chaos. The role for me, was always the same once I learned who had the dope, it was all over. I was the designated person to purchase the drugs. The main reason I purchased the dope is because I didn't trust anyone with my money and Rob vouched for me to his friends when it came to their money.

I can say though, that being around my family gave me a different outlet at times, which was refreshing. I could visit with my mom and my sisters often because all of them lived here in Denver.

The year now is 1989 and I find myself pregnant again and working at Samsonite. I go through trying to maintain sobriety and having a healthy baby. This is a good time to pause to share my addiction while being pregnant. I know that it was not good and certainly not for my child. There is no way to justify or even to help you understand what a living hell I went through knowing that I should not be smoking crack while I was pregnant. I prayed a lot during my pregnancies. I asked God to forgive me and to keep my kids from being affected by my stupidity and my addiction. Some of you, who are reading my story will attest to the stupidity but will not understand the addiction. Especially crack-cocaine. It is relentless on taking you down and out. It will kill you and it is only the Grace of God that saved me.

Alexandria LaSean is born on September 17, 1989, and she is a very beautiful and a healthy baby. She wasted no time in coming. My brother-in-law had to take me to the hospital because our car wouldn't start. On the way to the hospital Alexandria head started poking out. I was shouting, "Mike hurry, she's coming." Good thing we didn't have to go too far. When we got to the emergency room, the nurses kept telling me not to push. I tried but she did not want to wait. Alexandria came at about 5:00 a.m. After being in labor for forty-five minutes. Back then they would tie your tubes right then and there. So I had my tubes tied. As we would joke with a saying: "Tied, died, and burned to the side." At twenty-nine years old, I had made up my own mind, not to have any more children.

My mom took care of Alexandria while we worked. Alexandria was different from all the other children, I had had. Alex had my mom holding her all day or she would make their lives miserable by crying and when she came home with us, she would gladly sit in her swing or in her chair. She was the best baby ever. She acted older than she truly was.

On my twenty-ninth birthday, we (meaning my family) were sitting around watching a Bronco game and I yell to my son, for Anthony to check on Alexandria because she was in her basinet taking a nap. He yells back, "she's good. No more than twenty minutes later Rob goes in our room to check on her and he comes running out the room with Alexandria in his arms, crying that she is not breathing. I am shouting "no, no, not again! Rob is crying and shouting to call 911 and so I think I did, and they come and try to resuscitate her all the way to the hospital. I am crying and praying all at the same time. Asking God not to take her and making all kind of promises while feeling the worst I could feel. "Why God, on my birthday are you taking my baby. Why are you taking my baby girl, again? No! please let me have her," I cried. I couldn't understand why this was happening to us again. I felt so helpless and lost. I could feel all eyes on me, as if they were thinking how can we help her or what is she feeling? I just wanted to go in a closet and make life go away until I awaken from this bad dream.

My mom and sisters meet me at the hospital and my mom is trying to console me, but I am not feeling her or anyone else. After a while they allow me to go into the room with my daughter. She laid there lifeless and I felt so like, I don't know what's next. How do I survive after this? SIDS came to snatch another one of my daughter's. It was like life was playing a game with me and I was not winning. I sensed God, but not understanding why He allowed this to happen a second time.

The next day is Sunday and I am walking around in a daze but also trying to maintain in front of my other kids. Again, Anthony my oldest son understands and feels the pain of it all but my youngest two are not totally aware of what has happened. So my concern for Anthony heightens. Rob seems to be doing all right but he just doesn't understand why God would take the baby on my birthday. That stuck with him for a long time.

On Monday, we go to work (Rob and I both work at the same job, Samsonite) and what is so interesting is that when someone dies, people don't know what to say or how to console you and so it makes for a very difficult interaction with others. You want to say to them, "it's all right" but in your heart of hearts, you know it's not, but you want them to feel better about your lost. Death can be crazy, emotionally, but I am here to tell you that, God will take care of you.

Christmas was right around the corner and with us having to take care of the funeral and laying our baby to rest. There would be no money for Christmas presents for our children. About a week before Christmas, a truck pulls up at our house full of presents for our kids from our co-workers at Samsonite. It was so amazing. Our children had the best Christmas ever. Not only did they have gifts and toys, but we also had a Christmas feast with all the food donated. It was amazing!

Shortly after this the addiction was overtaking me again and I thought I could justify it because of the loss of my second child. I never really dealt with the loss of my two girls, but I don't think I had too because I knew God had dealt with me concerning them. It was for my good.

Note to self: Trust God always; he knows what's best for me.

Rob and I had a tough time getting along after this. We would argue over little stuff. I quit my job at Samsonite and our relationship became strained. We could not stand to be in the same room with each other. It got worse by the day and I had little reason to want to fix it.

One night I had taken the car to go purchase some crack with this woman and on the way, we got stopped by the cops and they claimed that I had a suspended license. They arrest me. For the first time in my life, I was going to jail at thirty years old and I was scared to death. The woman I was with promised that she would take my car home and that didn't happen. When the cops put the handcuffs on me, for the first time in my life I felt unsure about where this life was taking me. There was no conceivable way that my license should have been suspended. I had not been notified through the mail of a suspended license and I had not lived in Denver long enough for this to have happened.

The handcuffs are pinching me, and they are too tight and when I tell the cop, he is uninterested in loosening them. No compassion, heartless over a suspended license issue as if I was a full-blown criminal. Already I am seeing TV shows flash before my face if I was the starring bad guy.

I am here to tell you that the movies will mess you up about jail. It was bad but not that bad or maybe that's just Denver's jail. Anyways I cried, I think for the first hour and then I became a soldier. I thought I was too good to be there and that I didn't have any business being here. Wrong answer. I had every right to be here because whether I thought that I didn't belong, this time, was for all those times I should have been. I called my mom and she bonded me out, maybe within seven hours. When I was released the next day, my mom picked me up from jail. Rob was steaming about the car. I had to go look for the car and found it parked in a neighborhood called "Five Points." It's a wonder that the car was there untouched because this was not a very nice neighborhood. I didn't know much about all the hot spots in the Metro area except Montbello for drug activity, but this neighborhood had Montbello beat by a long shot. I had to call my mom and have her tow the car with her insurance.

Day by day the tension in our house was boiling over to the point of constant arguing. I felt this was not good on our children psyche. When I asked Rob to leave, he was dead set on not leaving. So as the weeks went by with no change, I decided to leave because I felt at this point anything is better than living in a house with a man who was mean and becoming hateful. I had already gone through this in my childhood and I was not ready to repeat history again. I explained to my kids that I would get better and get settled some-where else and they could then come with me. I went home weekly to see about my daughter's hair for a while and then that stopped as well because of transportation and the addiction. We made one attempt at trying to repair our marriage but me handing my unem-ployment check over to him was not something that I was willing to do, so I left again. A few months after that, Rob brings a woman to our house. I was so upset at him, I put my fist through the front window. Later, I would have a warrant for domestic violence because after I had left, he had called the cops on me. Somehow, through my mom I found out about this and I turned myself in and was released on my own recognizance (promise to return to future court dates).

Look, it was not an easy time for me leaving my children. I had been the parent that made sure they did their homework, brush their teeth, took baths and in the house before night fall. I was the one who was concerned about buying clothes and shoes, because this was not big on their daddy's list. He made sure they ate.

Street Life

My life has just gone from being a fulltime mom, wife and addict, to living wherever and being a fulltime crackhead. Most of the time, sleep was not happening because crack would not allow it and chasing it was now a twenty-four-hour, seven-days-a-week job. I watched the drug dealers and I learned who the addicts were.

This helped me to become the middleman and thus taking care of my own drug habit.

Montbello was where I hung out night and day. When I got so tired with nowhere to lay my head, I would retreat to either my mom's house or wait until Rob went to work and Anthony (my oldest son) would leave the back-door open so I could go to the basement where his bedroom was and I would go to sleep there. I would leave before Rob would get home.

My youngest sister had an apartment at the straight up crack spot, The Crossing (formerly known as The Lakes), where I was hanging out. I would run into her at times. Eventually she moved out and left me in her apartment because it was too much dope activity. This place jumped morning, noon and night. The cops' presence was always there. They rolled as much as we did. We learned their schedules for the most part. So eluding them was also a full-time job. We had lookouts and snitches. This world was crazy.

There was this one time that I had been up for seven days straight and I had gone into the apartment and laid on the floor and passed out. When I woke up, I didn't know where I was and how I got there. I didn't know what day it was. I started to cry because this was all so new to me and frankly it scared me to death. When I was a functional working addict, I never stayed up that many days. No sleep and very little food. There were times, I had to force myself to eat. Toting around my clothes in bags and leaving them sometimes, in a so-called friend's apartment or on someone's porch or balcony while I make my runs up and down the streets. I would try to look as normal as possible, not to attract the attention of the cops. That meant looking straight and not all highed up.

I met all kinds of people in this world of crack. Mothers, fathers, couples and a lot of single people living paycheck to paycheck for a crack high. They were falling like me. The next crack rock was more important than paying a bill. I saw couples fight over their last dollar. I saw couples split up due to one addiction worse than the other. I saw single people letting dope dealers sit in their house and sell dope until the dope dealer got tired of giving all his dope away to the person's house he was at. It was "on the move activity" for the drug dealer, to eliminate them from getting busted and that's why it was important to have runners (the less people the drug dealer had to deal with the better). That's what I did. I would get people and bring them or their money to the dealer and purchase the dope for them. I would then get my cut either from the dealer or the person I was coping, for. I would then take my portion, sell it or smoke it and wait for the next person to come along.

I hung out with the guys more than the women because the women were more into prostituting and that was not my cup of tea. One time I did get busted for "pimping and pandering" but never prostitution and that charge was a bunch of hog wash because I was just with the chick who was prostituting.

Side note: this did not make me no better than the prostitute because there were times that sleeping around with a guy who was buying all the crack was essential to staying off the streets, especially on sting days. (days where cops would set up sting operations to catch prostitutes and sometimes dope dealers and runners).

Everybody will not tell you everything but there were things that the women crackheads knew about men crackheads. That was when they got high nine out of ten men couldn't do crap sexually once they took that first hit. Nature wouldn't allow it.

Anyway, I could outsell any of these guys. For one, I considered myself honest and I was smart. If you did the people right, they would come looking for you when they needed more. Most of the crackheads (that's what they called us who was strung out on crack), I hung with, believed in ripping off everyone, including me, if I didn't stay alert. How they survived was beyond me. Most of them didn't. There was a lot of beatings for running off with some dope dealer's dope. There were even people dying and never hearing from them again. Another thing I didn't believe in doing. If I messed up, I wouldn't hide I would go and confess up. Then I would run dope for them for free, until I made up the loss.

Side note: The dope dealers were mostly gang members, such as the Crips and the Bloods. They were just getting strong when I hit the streets in 1990 in Denver and Aurora.

Crackheads would hide out and put other people lives in jeopardy because of their thieving ways. (This story happened much later in my life on the street, but it seems appropriate to tell it now). There was this one time when I was on my way to a crack smoking house, when I got in the stairway out of view of the street in an apartment complex that sits on Joliet and Sixteenth Avenue, this guy dressed like a ninja rushed up behind me with a gun in my back and made me knock on the door and when they opened it he pushed me in and told me and this other girl, that was already there, to get on the floor. His entire face was covered except for his eyes. He had black on from head to toe. He took pillows and put them over our heads. At that moment I just knew it was over. You talk about praying and scared all at the same time wondering if they were going to shoot us in the head, this was me. We heard another guy come in too. They took the person who lived there into the bathroom and they were screaming at him about their money and their dope. They sound like they were smashing his hand with something liked a hammer and the reason I know that is because they kept yelling for him to put his hand down on the vanity. It was so intense. They told us if we looked from underneath those pillows, they would kill us. They told him if he didn't get their money to them, they were coming for him. They gave him a deadline. Suddenly, it was if they moved light on their feet and gone just as quick as they came. I could barely hear them, rushing pass us. They opened the window and jumped out the window. I remember peeking from under the pillow, after about a couple minutes of dead silence, I didn't see anybody I jumped up and ran out the front door with the other girl on my heels, like two gazelles running for their lives. Now, anybody in their right mind would have said, "Hell no," to this life and turned straight after this scene, right out of the movies type scene. I wondered if being a crackhead was worth it and the next hit of dope talked me right back into staying. This is one of those times I wanted to give up but no sooner than we had run down the street to get away, the girl that I had been laid out on the floor with, her man had crack waiting for us. After that day, I never saw Lisa again. She was the young woman in the room with me that day. I had to sit down after this for a moment to thank God, for saving me.

My hangout spot in Montbello was on Albrook Dr. in the Crossings Apartments. I had a guy friend that I used to hang out at his place. I knew quite a few apartments to hang out in. One day, there was this chick who townhouse I would go by on a regular basis. She seemed as if she was on the up and up until I took one of my customer's over to her house.

I had dropped him off so that he had a place to get high. I also had left my coat over at her house because it had been nice outside, and I hadn't had a real need to wear it. It was right after the Christmas of 1990. I remembered it because my oldest sister, Kim had bought me a white winter coat. I guess she knew I needed one being out there on the streets. I fell in love with that coat. So anyway, after dropping my guy customer over this chick's house, I went back later to sit and get high too, but she would not let me in. So I kept knocking on the door.

Eventually she got tired of me knocking and she opened the door and started yelling at me. That's when I told her to give me my coat. She would not and slammed the door. Then I could hear them inside telling me to get away from the house. When I did not leave, she came outside with a knife in her hand and started trying to stab me with it. She stabbed me in my chest, and I ran off and called the police. They came and arrested her, and the ambulance took me off to the hospital. I was at Denver General Hospital because it was a trauma hospital. They had to run dye through me to make sure my lung was not punctured. That was excruciating pain.

I had fallen asleep and when I woke up, half my family was standing around my bed. My husband and kids also came. I didn't like the idea of my kids seeing me this way. I went home with them after spending a couple of days in the hospital. Close call. This should have stopped me from ever going back out there again but when I found out that they had extradited her back to the state where she had a warrant, I felt safe enough to go back out.

Venturing to the apartments down the street known as the Devonshire Apartments was now my new hangout place. My guy friend had moved down here as well. We tried being a couple, but he had issues (alcohol and crack) and it didn't make for a stable relationship. Alcohol and crack mixed would turn out bad on all levels of abuse. He would get drunk and have his friends over and that did not make for a good combination. He got belligerent one too many times. I would be like "I gotta go, see you later." One of those times he kicked me and I left his apartment and went and called the cops on him because I remembered that my mama said, "if a man put his foot on you, that was a strong indication that he has no love for you."

On another occasion when Friday evening came, it was considered "get your money night." All the people who worked and smoked crack were clear targets for this night. Some of the dudes though, were not into the drugs, they just wanted sex. So this one night I couldn't catch anyone that wanted crack, so I pursued getting one of the dudes who was looking for sex in hopes that I could turn them on to some drugs. I ran across this one guy who had no interest in the crack but took me for a prostitute and I took him to be a trick, for real. I played the game well and I winded up with him buying me some crack, food and going to his place to have sex. Everything happened but the sex. I ate my food and smoked my crack until he couldn't keep his eyes open any longer due to him being too drunk when I ran into him earlier that night. I had watched him put his money up in the top of the closet and so this to me was going to be one of those times that many women talked about concerning their "tricks" but I had never experienced something like this. His first mistake was taking me for a whore and two, him being too drunk to know his own name. So after he passed out, I made my move for the closet and took his whole paycheck. I took off out the door straight to the crack house. The next day they came looking for me. I was standing on the balcony at a friend's apartment when they spotted me. They pile out of their vehicles and started shouting and accusing me of taking the money, but I denied it. (The complex that they stayed in was right next to the one I hung out in.) Stupid move. I was like "Did you see me take it?"

They kept saying that I was the only one there, and I kept denying it, so eventually they left because of the scene that it started to create. This was one of the three times that I stole something from somebody. I was not going to make that a habit because dying was not on my agenda. I loved me. Then why would I put myself in situations to get killed? The need to stay sedated so I didn't have to see how bad I was screwing up my life. I realize that coping with life was not that bad but the need to have someone love you, is. So I thought.

Note to self: You just need the right kind of love. Love yourself.

The next time I stole something almost got me killed. Again, it was a Friday night and I was working for this one gang member and I was making him a lot of money. He would give me about a twenty-dollar rock of crack every hundred dollars I brought to him. Early in the morning after business had slowed down, I went to the apartment where all of them were laid around sleep. I knock and the door was slightly open, so I went in. I shook him and asked him to sell me a rock and he yelled at me and told me, "B——ch, get out."

He turned over and dropped his whole dope sack and I picked it up and walked out the door. I was hiding out for two days getting high. I told my guy friend what had happened and how the gang member had called me out my name after all the business I had brought him. Well, a week went by and the gang member saw me and called me over to the apartment. I went in and he told me to come to the back to the bedroom and I did. Once in there, he started asking me about the sack of dope. He told me if I lied, he would kill me. I told him why, I took it and all of a sudden, other gang members started coming out of nowhere into the room and they started hitting me and kicking me. I am now covering up my face. After a few minutes they stop and the main one is standing me up and telling me to open my mouth. He sticks a gun in my mouth, and he pulls the trigger. Nothing happens. I start praying and asking God to save me. He pulls the trigger again and again nothing happens. My heart is racing. I am scared out of my mind wondering if these fools are really hardened criminals.

Next thing I know there is a commotion at the bedroom door and their girlfriends, show up and push them aside and yell "Jackie run, run Jackie run. I break loose and I haul tail out of there and I run to find a place that they would not know of, to hide out. I learned that in all of that they said Mike told them. Mike is my guy friend; best friend and he was a drunk. So I can imagine him and his drunk butt telling them. They didn't even ask him; he had offered the information to them. That's why it took them a week to confront me. I couldn't believe that I had come this close to dying. How could Mike have been so crude to rat me out. In the back of my mind, I thought that if the time presented itself, he would get his just reward, because this drunk would eventually let his guard down and I would return the favor to empty his pockets. By the way, I did get the opportunity to empty his pockets about two months later because he got drunk.

A couple of hours went by and the gang member sent someone looking for me with a message and promised that he would not hurt me. I was reluctant but I knew that if I was going to keep walking around this place I had to find out if they were going to be after me. To my surprise, he kept his word and explained to me that he had to do what he did because of the pressure from California heads (leaders). He gave me more dope to keep running for him, but I knew that it was time to give this scene up. The business relationship had been damaged and it could not be repaired. All the dope in the world could not erase what they had done to me that day. He was not to be trusted again. Shame on me the first time and a second time was not going to be "shame on you." You gotta know when God is sending you help, and I recognized my "God moments" in spite of, my need to be all highed up.

About a couple of weeks later I had to change my location. I ventured out to Colfax and Oswego area. Life was not easy out here in these streets. After that last battle, I would now try and be more careful. I had to learn a whole new area. The crackheads were not the same and fitting in was never easy because some of the crackheads were far more scandalous beyond anything that I had ever experienced before. See, what I could never wrap my mind around was the fact that the crackhead runners should have been the greater force on the streets but they had a strange mentality (it's all about me) but it should have been "let's put our heads together and we can run these streets because we are the ones with the customers, not the dealers." Don't think for one moment that I didn't try to relay this with a few of them but in the end, it would always lead back to "it's all about me." Every crackhead for themselves.

I played the game the best I could and tried to have some sense of integrity amongst my fellow crackheads. They played, "Let's see how many people I can get today." I started to see fake crack rocks. We call fake crack rock "woo." I've seen people roll up on a car and hand them a real rock (not a crack rock) but a straight up real rock off the ground and take their money and dare the person to come back and confront them. Every now and again we would hear of someone getting their tails kicked because they sold somebody some "woo." There was a lot of shady characters in these streets. We all knew who was almost legit, kind of shady and the down-right dirty to the bone and those of us crackheads, didn't fool around with them. It was best to leave those fools alone if you wanted to live to see another day.

Drug movies that I had watched in the past were becoming really real in my life. As I am thinking about it now, it was pretty scary knowing that I must have been out of my mind to have put myself in that much danger.

Most of us working out in the street daily would be up for days at a time. I think my longest was nine and a half days before I would pass out. Surely you better be in a good place when you pass out because you wouldn't have your shoes or anything of value when you woke up. I remember passing out in a crackheads apartment with people who I thought had my back but when I woke up everything was gone. Dope, pipes, money, and even my coat. When I asked where my stuff was, they threw me out of their apartment. Lesson learned.

One time I had been up for seven days and I was walking down Colfax and I fell asleep and the only thing that kept me from dying that day was, I stepped off the curb and immediately I woke up. That was the most scariest thing ever happen to me while just walking down the street. I was so afraid if I didn't get somewhere to lay down, next time I could be stepping in front of a car. So I started crying and looking for somewhere to lay down. I found this little church and it had an aluminum boat in the driveway and I crawled under it and went to sleep. It was the most peaceful sleep I had gotten in a long time.

I don't exactly know what year I first got busted with crack, but it was not nice. It was somewhere around 1994, I had about three crack rocks on me and some marijuana. I was walking in one of the motel's parking lot near Kingston on Colfax. This car had just drove into the parking lot. I was thinking to myself, *They might want some crack.* Come to find out they were asking me if I knew a certain person who lived there? Before I could answer them, this cop car barrels into the parking lot.

The cop jumps out of his car and ask me what am I doing and when I tell him that I am helping these people find their family member who lived there, the cop ask me another question before I could finish answering the first one. What is in your hand? I immediately throw the crack on the ground and he grabs me by my arm and throws me to the ground. My face is in pain, after hitting the parking lot surface and I can sense that I am bleeding. He becomes more violent and stuffs his knee in my back. I am yelling that he is hurting me, and he doesn't even seem to care. They literally throw me into the back of the squad car. The people who were looking for their relative was stunned. Just like me. I get arrested and charged with my first dope case.

After seeing my public defender, she wants to fight my case on the law of "right to be left alone." I was not visually doing anything illegal and they rolled up on me because of it being the middle of the night or they had been watching me stroll on the Fax (that's what we called the street named Colfax). I could not fight the case because I could not bond myself out and I was not willing to sit in jail until the trial. So I pleaded guilty. I received probation. I had to report to a probation officer. That did not go well, because no one told me that I had to report to the probation office. This was my first rodeo with the court system and dumbfounded, was I. I eluded the cops for a while.

After being on the run for a month, I had been in Montbello and I was looking for a ride back over to the Colfax and Joliet area. This man offered me a ride. What I didn't notice when I got in the car is that there was no handle to get out of the passenger side. I begin to think that something is not right. So when we turned off Peoria onto Twenty-Sixth Avenue. He began to tell me that he wanted sex and that he was not going to pay for it. I am like "ok.?" Knowing in my mind that I must find the right moment to run.

So he pulls over in an abandon area by Stapleton Airport. I suggest that we get in the back seat and so when he lets me out, he walks around the car to get in on the other side and as I open the back door on the passenger's side, I pretend I am going to get in and I take off running. He gets back in the driver side and comes after me in his no handle tricked-out car. I duck behind some bushes. I see this fool frantically trying to find me as he is zooming up and down the streets. I make a mad dash toward this house that has a light on, and I knock on the door in a frantic. This white older lady answers the door and I tell her that I have to use the bathroom really bad. She lets me in, and I tell her that somebody is following me. She looks at me intently and I am thanking her for letting me come in. After she senses that I am harmless she offers me something to eat and drink and she asked if I wanted to call the police. I said, "no." I couldn't call the cops because I don't know if I have a warrant out for my arrest due to me not reporting to probation. After sitting there for thirty minutes, I leave, and I thanked her for her hospitality. I am sort of scared but also knowing that I could not sit in this woman's house to long.

I have this man's wallet with his ID, and I throw it down in the gutter. I should have turned him in. I thought to myself, how many women had he gotten into his no handle trick-out car and made them have sex with him? Thank God! I was not one of them. I sensed that no matter what I had gone through, God was with me.

After this I decided that I would turn myself in to my probation officer and I did. She gave me another chance and free again I was. I believe that I went home to my mom's house for a little while. I got good and rested before going back out to the streets again.

This time I moved to the Colfax and Beeler area. I met new druggies and it was getting more creative with the stunts they pulled. It seemed as if the further I moved down Colfax the more treacherous it got. I began to see people that I used to get high with from Montbello. One of the crackheads (I will call him D) who was a runner like me, had a spot (drug house) on Beeler and we all hung out there. This house went day and night mainly with smokers and alcoholics. Evidently, this was D's, daddy's apartment and his mama who had a house in Montbello with her current husband, also hung out at this house too with her ex-husband. Strange relationships.

Note to wives: If you are still talking to your ex, make sure it's just talks.

I guess it was several months that I would be in and out of this spot. One day, I had been in and out of there a lot and D's daddy had wanted a pint of liquor. So because I had money and wanted to hang out there, I bought him a pint. It was some serious crack smoking and liquor drinking going on this night. I needed to get some air (you could cut the air with a knife because there was so much smoke) so I left and the next morning I stop back by and there was cops everywhere. Come to find out D's daddy had been rushed to the hospital where he had died of cirrhosis of the liver. I cried and cried because I had bought his last pint of liquor and I had no idea that that man had a bad liver. This spot was shut down after this. Sad time.

I decided to move on down the road around Colfax and Verbena. I am still on probation, but I had never ever shown up for probation after meeting with my probation officer the first time. I never adhered to taking UA's (urine analysis) or anything. In other words, I was totally defiant. I believe some of it stemmed from lack of knowledge and not understanding the system and the repercussions.

I am at one of the crack motels on Valentia St. and the woman whose room I was at, had asked me to go to the store. I am walking across the street and a cop stopped me for j-walking when I really wasn't because I was crossing over in a cross walk (this is how the cops treated you, if you were a regular known druggie. They just make up a reason, even if you weren't doing anything. When they arrested me, I told them my sister's name and so as I was laying in the city jail, they called out my real name and I knew I was not getting out, no time soon. They transferred me to Arapahoe County Jail and there I stayed until I went to court. The Judge wanted to give me Community Corrections which is the halfway house but I had heard war stories about them so I asked the judge to send me to DOC (prison) and he said, "Are you sure about this Jacqueline," and I said "I am." So he sentenced me to four years DOC… I served 364 days between county jail and actual prison, one day, shy of a year.

Life in prison was a piece of cake and nothing like what I had seen on TV. It was more of a daycare for women. Women guards watching women inmates. Everybody for the most part was too busy trying to be with another woman, that they did not have time to fight and keep up a lot of mess. I did miss my freedom and knowing that I just couldn't get up and walk out was the worst feeling ever. Knowing that you have an out date does not make it any easier on the time that you have, to do. One day locked up feels like a lifetime. I called my mom maybe every other month. This is when I asked my mom for some scripture to get me through and she gave me the Twenty-Third Psalm (The Lord is my Shepherd).

Note to you: Recognize your God moments. They will see you through and keep your fire kindled until…

My job in prison was on the construction school crew in Canon City. I learned how to stucco a wall. Pretty interesting. I forgot the pay (probably $2.25 a week) but it was never enough but, I had everything I needed, because God had a way of turning a little into a lot. After about six months in Canon City, they transferred me to minimum security facility in Pueblo, Colorado. I stayed there about three months until I paroled to my mom's house.

I had to wear an ankle bracelet when I got paroled. I applied for a job at a frozen warehouse and I got the job (receiving clerk), mainly because I knew someone who knew someone but all in all, it was God. Thirty days out, I get arrested for a case in Jefferson County. I was sick about it. "Why didn't they do their job to find out if everything was clear when they released me from prison," I thought.

I am sitting in Jeffco county jail wondering if I am going to lose my job and lose my confidence in things that I had been achieving thus far. I stayed in there one week because when I went to court the District Attorney didn't have their paperwork together. This was one of my God moments because I prayed the whole time, I was in there. The judge declared time served and let me return on ISP (ankle bracelet). What should have lasted one year (on the ankle bracelet), was over in three months. My parole officer let me go. Praise God! is all I could say.

I had my job back as a receiving clerk for the frozen food warehouse. Two years later I am feeling on top of the world concerning my sobriety and the productive lifestyle that I am leading, but still feeling the void in my life that I have felt all my life. There could be a room full of people and as long as everyone was good, I was good, so I thought. Something was missing and I couldn't put my finger on it.

Staying with my mom and stepdad wasn't too bad. One day they were watching TV and the movie they were watching was "Joseph" with Ben Kingsley. I never really liked Bible movies except the Ten Commandments with Charleston Heston, because they were doing too much (maybe too much was the made-up stuff). This movie however got my attention quickly and I sat down with them to watch it. Something came over me as I watched it and I told God I wanted to be like Joseph. I think he heard me. I didn't think much about it after that. But that day something ignited in me. It was almost if I had gotten a revelation in my spirit but again, I couldn't put my finger on it.

Work was interesting enough but one day a truck driver came in who was into drugs. We got to talking and I went with him after work. I got a taste of what I had stayed away from for two years and now to let all that go down the drain was not good. After hanging out with him and getting high, he ran out of money and I was sort of glad because I knew I should get home so no one would think that I was up to no good. I got home late, but not late enough that my mom questioned me. I went on as if nothing happened. It did affect me though. It reminded me of what it was like to be getting high all over again. I was just glad no one had found me out. This one time had me thinking about it all over again.

I had the pressures of life and everybody wanting something from me now that I was making a decent living. Working is a drag, when your whole check is going to everyone else but you. I wanted to run to get away from everybody. Payday came along and all day I played with the thoughts in my mind. I got on the bus and it was like I was fighting a devil on one shoulder and an angel on the other. The crack devil won the first round. The closer the bus got to an old hang out spot the more I got bubble gut for the crack. Bubble gut is when your stomach and mind connect that crack is about to be ingested in one form or another and you must find a bathroom quickly. I got a motel room and stayed out in the streets. Life doesn't change on the streets. It's the same old games and I hadn't got tried enough to stop. The adrenaline was still flowing and hotter than before. Once you have had a battle and get clean, and return, it gets more intense then the last time.

It was only a little time after going back out that I get stopped (walking in the parking lot) at a gas station on Colfax and Valentia. I had called one of my dope dealers to meet me at this gas station. She shows up and so do undercover cops too. They drive up on me and immediately started searching me and they find a pipe on me and arrest me for paraphernalia. My thought is this; how can you buy a pipe but can't possess a pipe? Backward laws. They arrested her too, but I don't understand why? The cops take us to a holding tank on Colorado Blvd. While we are in the tank, she asked me to take the dope out of her bra and throw it in the toilet. Now, I was feeling some kind of way because in my head I am thinking, "Don't do that" and on the other hand, I am feeling like "help her get rid of her drugs." When I lean over to do it like a fool, the cops rush in and separate us and they take her dope. They were charging me for her dope. They take us to county jail and this heifer is telling everyone that I got her busted and if I did why am I getting charged with her dope. I called my mom as soon as I got to the county jail. My mom then called her friend and they bonded me out. They did it because they believed me. This time I hired me a lawyer.

I stayed clean for a minute, but it didn't last long. I collected unemployment for a while from my previous job and it was the resource to me taking care of my addiction once again.

This time out cost me, and not that every time before didn't, but this one hurt to the core. I was walking down the street on Yosemite, all highed up. Looking for someone who wanted to buy some crack. These young boys were walking toward me, and I spoke like in a question mark kind of way. Then as they passed, I sort of sensed that I knew one of them. My memory had left me. I turned around to say, "Don't I know you?" The one boy said, "Yeah, I am Caster," and I felt so done because here is my child walking pass me and I didn't even know who he was. I didn't know what to say and so I made small talk and told him not to be out here in these streets. As I walk away feeling so low, ashamed and tears running down my face, I am thinking on how I look and what must be going through his mine and his friends' mine, seeing his Mom looking like this cracked out hoe (whether you hoe or not this is what they call you on the street when crack is all you live for). At that moment, I knew I was screwed up. A changed had to come soon.

It all came to a halt in January of 2000 when I get busted again with a twenty-dollar rock of crack. Let me give you heads up about the way of the street. All dope dealers most of the time are leery of the white man and thinking they are the po-po but I got busted by an undercover black man. Go figure.

This time I am so done with myself because now I can see that something must change. Two dope cases and who would save me this time. I was arrested, taken to court and the District Attorney was a black lady and she was recommending sixteen to thirty-two years in prison. What in the world is going on? You would have thought I did something to someone else to deserve this much time. So my lawyer had work to do. I sit in jail while waiting for my sentencing date. Long days and even longer nights, waiting and wondering what would happen now. The night before court, I prayed fervently for God to help me out of this ordeal that was not going to turn out good if He didn't step in. The next day in court, my lawyer shows up and I did not see the District Attorney. My lawyer comes over to me and tell me that the district attorney that was trying to crucify me was not in court and that another, woman district attorney was in her place.

He told me that this was our chance to see if she would be willing to recommend to the judge an in-patient drug rehab for two years. The district attorney agreed and so the judge gave me two years, in Stout Street Foundation, which is a drug rehab. When the judge sentenced me, I cried like a baby, I was so happy and praising God for coming through for me, one more time. I decided I was not going to waste this time. I knew in my mind that I did not want to face another court date ever. Having someone deciding your fate is not a nice space to be in, but when you have Jesus Christ on your side everything is possible. A couple of weeks later Stout Street came to pick me up from the county jail.

Rehab was never what I expected. It separated the men from the women in living quarters and it presented an environment that was very disciplined. There was a time schedule that you had to adhere to. It was also a working rehab. I got my therapy while working because everyone was watching you. When you break a rule then you would spend time on the bench (sitting on a bench for however many of hours of the infraction). Do you know how hard it is to sit on a bench and not be able to talk to people walking by or to anyone sitting on the bench with you? It's pretty hard. In the long run, it was all worth it. There were people there from all walks of life. Poor people, rich people, white people, black people, spanish people and Asian people. Addiction does not care to miss you because of color, culture or stature. Some were sentenced and some just came on their own. Many times, those that were sentenced would just get up and leave without the regard of being caught. If you left and you were sentenced there, you would get a case of escape. For me that was not an option. I was determined to finish this so that I could get on with my life. I was getting up in age, thirty-nine to be exact and life was passing me by, and I had not accomplished much. Everything good that I had ever started was never being completed. I was living out what my dad had pronounced over my life. Little did I know that I was writing my story as I walked it out. I was determined to change the ending.

About a month in the rehab, this young man (I don't use the word "young" loosely, seven years younger than me) started trying to holla at me. His name was Rodney.

Now one of the rules in Stout Street was no relationships. This could give you major consequences. Those consequences being thirty days standing on your feet working and eight hours on the bench.

Rodney would write me letters and sneak them to me in several ways. Secrets are necessary.

I had a little talk with God before this ever occurred and I was telling God that if, "You can send me somebody or not, whatever You think is best for me, I accept." Besides, I was not willing to go back to my husband and my husband had already started searching for him a new wife. Too many bridges had been burnt in our relationship. We were still on talking terms and that was good enough for the both of us and besides we had kids together, so that was a bond that could not be broken. In July of 2000, the divorce papers were drawn up and my mom brought them to me at the rehab. I did not contest it and I did not cry. The other thing was, I was going to have to change my choices in men. It's bad when your spouse only thinks of themselves. If my husband had loved me, like he loved himself, I believe we could have made it through this.

Note to dating people: Selfishness will not work on any level.

Rodney was so the opposite, of what I had experienced in the past. He was looking for a relationship that would lead to love. I questioned God if "He had sent him." I didn't get a definite answer, so I let Rodney pursue me.

We kept our distance in the rehab but smiled at each other on a sly. There were different activities at the rehab. We had a softball team that we played other institutions. So we were all at a softball game and I remember playing third base. Now, Rodney and I were both on the softball team. This guy from the other team gets up to bat and he line drives the ball straight at me, and I held out my left hand to catch the ball and I did, but then fell to my knees in pain because it had come with such force that it sprained my forefinger. I looked over at the dugout and Rodney had a tear streaming down his cheek and I fell in love, at that very moment. I know that sounded a little corny but that's what happened. Compassion is too often absent in men, so to see a man display compassion in front of others is big on my list of character traits.

Rodney's job at the rehab was driving the residents around to different facilities within the organization. So he was elected to take me to the hospital. No one knew at the time that he liked me and I him. We kept it on the low, low. We talked at the hospital. This was one of the first times having a real conversation. There were other times like being allowed to go to Church on Sundays. We even got baptized at the Church, while being in the rehab.

A couple of months go by and I am working in the telemarketing department and Rodney being a driver was always delivering to different facilities of the rehab. He also could use the phone. He calls over to the TM department and I answer but little did I know one of the directors had picked up the phone the same time I did and heard our conversation. Next thing I know the director is calling me downstairs. He escorts me over to the main office and tells me to sit on the bench. I look up and they are now escorting Rodney in and tell him to sit on the bench too. At that very moment, I knew we had been busted. I was relieved, for the stress of hiding and sneaking around was getting old.

The counselors talked to both of us before they gave us our consequences. Besides giving us the consequence of standing on our feet to work for thirty days and eight hours on the bench. They added a communication ban too. We could no longer talk to each other. So the next year and a half was still sneaking around to talk. The rehab was so dead set against us talking that they decided to ask me to go up to Estes Park to the rehab's ranch to finish out my first part of my program with a young lady (I'll call her Dina) that needed to be incognito.

Estes Park is where I failed myself. I should have embraced this beautiful place, but I was too focused on the director who I will call Mac, who was in charge of the ranch and his dislike for me. I wanted off that mountain and to be back in Denver. I did like the fact that it was just me and her in the women's house. It was built for two. The men had a house about a thousand yards away and much bigger. We would wake up in the morning and big Elk would be hanging out all over the ranch. It was so amazing and up here I could sense God but again I failed to embrace His presence.

There were all kinds of cool animal life up here and I loved that part of it. We got our therapy through working and keeping the ranch cleaned. Mac didn't come around too often but when he did, he was a thorn in my side. We would have these therapeutic games and he would use the games to talk crazy to us. I didn't consider that therapeutic then but as I look back it helped me to take what was mine and let all else go. He had us doing hard labor. Cleaning gullies and ditches and whatever else he could come up with. I was so fed up with Mac's antics, that Dina and I made phone calls back to the Denver facility, to get other directors to come get us. But it wasn't until we got the Founder of the rehab on the phone, were we allowed to come back. He personally came up to Estes to take us back to Denver.

I went to the next phase of my program called "re-entry and so did Rodney who I was glad to see. Three months seemed like a life-time in Estes Park but all worth it.

In Re-entry, there was no communication ban and so we began dating. It was fun and a headache all at the same time. Everybody still, watching us. They acted like they had not seen two people in love. After enough of the harassment by the staff, Rodney left the program because he was one of the ones who was not court ordered.

Rodney got an apartment and I would come over early in the morning to his apartment before going to work. I had acquired a good telemarketing job apart from Stout Street. I moved from tele-marketing representative to supervisor in two weeks.

While working at Stout Street and this new outside job, I am now starting to find out, what some of my strengths are. So many things are transforming in my life now. It was like an awakening. I had been getting high for so long that now that I am sober, I am real-izing that there was more to me than I had realized before.

What I would like to convey is that, I had been getting high since I was eighteen years old and now, I am forty-one and only one other time did I have a two-year break from crack, but this time is different because I have gotten older, wiser and tired of living life with no meaning and purpose. All the times before during my func-tional days working a job, I was still high off, marijuana but now I am totally drug free. It feels real good.

I get my driver license back while I am in the rehab. I graduated from Stout Street Foundation and I move in with Rodney. This is the first time in my adult life that there are no drugs, not even mar-ijuana. So going to work, coming home to cook dinner, watch TV and spending time with the person who was loving me and I him, routine is okay, especially when there are no drugs.

Note to Addict: When all the substances are gone don't look for the wrong thing to take its place, because that's what the former addict does.

Rodney and I began to talk about getting married, but we also talk about me not being able to have any more children either. In spite of that, he still wanted to marry me. This should have sent up red flags for me, but I loved the fact that Rodney was loving on me. He wanted kids too bad though. On September the thirteenth, which was a Friday, 2002, we go to the justice of the peace and get married. After getting married, we try to find us a Church home, but we were not consistent enough. Still life was moving right along. We would go out together to dinner and movies, something I didn't do in my previous marriage. Taking a walk in the park was even nice with Rodney. Our first Christmas together was good, getting to know each other and really settling into doing life together. We decided to move into a bigger apartment from the little studio that we had been living in. This is when my daughter who had been living with her grandmother came to live with Rodney and me. She was in her last year of high school and about to graduate. The time is now April of 2003.

One day I come home from work and Rodney is getting high off marijuana and drinking a drink. My heart leaps of out of my chest and I am having flashbacks to my drugging days. I ask him what the world do you think you are doing after all the rehab we have gone through? I don't even remember how he answered me, but I know it wasn't a satisfactory answer because now in a moment of time, drugs once more is about to consume our lives. I was not trying to do drugs anymore. Rodney was my drug. I forgot the note to addict, 'cause now I am replacing the substance, with a man.

It didn't take long for us to be just as dysfunctional and out of control as when we had entered the rehab.

I began to finally figure out that a person who is not content with life or they can't find meaning and purpose in life, will often times revert right back to the dysfunctional behavior to not have to cope with anything else.

This time around I just wanted to enjoy life with my husband without the outside influences. My kids are all grown now and all the past mistakes I made concerning them and everything else was behind me now and a new beginning is all I longed for.

It didn't take long for the marijuana turning into the need for a stronger high. Crack was back and I was wondering how could this be so. I went through all the reasons why I could not afford to do crack anymore, all the time still puffing on the pipe. It was ludicrous. We chased it for one month and then on Sunday, May 18, 2003, we had been getting high all day in a hotel because we didn't want to be around my daughter. My mom was trying to get in touch with me to tell me she would be moving to Yuma, Arizona, with my brother. I was so high, I couldn't talk with her and told her I would call her back. I then had a conversation with Rodney about getting away from Denver because I couldn't take this drug life not one more day.

He thought about all I was saying and on the next morning before my brother and mom pulled out, I called her and told her our situation concerning the drugs and how we were all out of money, but we had to go. She told us that she would pay for our gas and to load up our truck and let's hit the road. My brother and mom met us at the gas station and filled up our truck and we were leaving our life behind here in a moment's notice. It was that crucial to me, but I didn't like leaving my daughter again. That part hurt real bad but, I had to save my life, or I wouldn't have one to tell of.

We left the apartment in the hands of my eighteen-year-old daughter and didn't look back. So on May 19, 2003, we leave Colorado. As I look back now, this was so irresponsible and hard to swallow. So many unanswered questions and a lot of loose ends. Have you ever dropped everything without thinking and left it all behind?

Note to self: Don't ever think this is cool but necessary.

Spiritual Awakening

Seeing Arizona again was good and exciting because I loved the warmer weather, but I did not anticipate the oven of Yuma. Yuma is, 120 degrees in the daylight and 100 at night. No relief from the heat.

We quickly find jobs. My first job there is telemarketing and Rodney is working in a nursing home. We are living with my brother and my mom and life is normal again.

From here, life must get better. We search out a Church because we know we must get grounded in Jesus Christ, and He would certainly be our saving grace. Jesus would show us how to do life and how to do it sober. Union Missionary Baptist Church is where we land, and it was good.

Everything is going good but we are still addicted to cigarettes and they must go too. We start looking for a place of our own. We find a cute little apartment, not far from my mom and brother although Yuma is not that big anyway. When we moved there, you could go from one side of town to the other in ten minutes.

Our one-year anniversary is coming up soon and so we decide to go to San Diego to celebrate before our anniversary. San Diego is only one hour and forty-five minutes away from Yuma. Now while we are there, we give up smoking cigarettes. We spend three days there, bowling and checking out different restaurants, just having some relaxation time.

When we get back that same week, which is the first week in September of 2003, Rodney decides not to come home this one night. I am calling him, and he is making every excuse why he is not home. So he says he is out having a beer with a co-worker, but

Rodney doesn't have any friends, but it could have been a co-worker. So I let that fly over my head and I go to bed. When I wake up to go to work the next morning, he's still not home. So I call him, and he say he is on his way home. I get dressed and he is still not home. I call him again and he again tells me he is on his way home and this time I get really upset and tell him I got to be at work in ten minutes. I don't suspect anything at this moment because truly I am feeling that Rodney is on the same page I am on, concerning drugs.

Fifteen minutes later he shows up and he is acting funny, but I wasn't really paying attention. I get in my truck and as I am driving, it dawns on me that he had been acting funny, like getting high funny. I turn the truck around and go back home and he is getting high. I ask him if he had any more and he said "no." So I tell him to let's go get some more. That quick everything changed for me. I did not know that it was that easy to fall right back into this crazy addiction. I don't know why this thing is still plaguing our lives, but it was. We go get more and it is September 4, 2003, and little did we know what lied ahead of us.

This time was different than any other time that I had ever smoked crack before. When smoking crack for most people your senses of alertness is heighten, but I am here today to tell you that the atmosphere was strange. I guess a way of putting it is, there was a presence as if we were not alone. It was a presence of peace and if someone was watching over us (you would have had to been there). Why was someone watching over us this time? Our awareness went to a whole new level. One person said to me "oh you two were just hallucinating," I have never seen any pink elephants or anything else that was not real, just for the record.

While we are getting high, we also read scripture out of the Bible. Our mission is deliverance this time, I guess. In the past, I always used to pray for protection and for God to provide food and a place to stay and He always did. We need, I need this addiction gone forever, I pray. By now, I have reached a level of tiredness. This addiction is getting old and I want out. That is what is in my spirit.

I call off from work for the next week. I don't even know why I thought I needed that many days but oh well, it was on and cracking, if you get my drift. One night we are sitting in the bathroom getting high because there were no windows and when a person is smoking crack, you always want to not be flicking a lighter by windows. Suspicious activity is a good way to get you busted. So we avoided windows at all cost. We are in the bathroom and all of a sudden, we hear talking like if somebodies were on the roof over the bathroom talking through the air vent. We clearly heard them say, "They are getting high."

Rodney says to me, "Did you hear those angels?"

I was like "Yeah," and looking like, what in the world is going on? Rodney and I immediately put everything away and go outside to look up on the roof and there was no one there. We went back in the house and we began discussing what we just heard. It was clear as day. We sense that we are surrounded by angels. So we take a break to change rooms. We go in the living room and we spread a blanket out on the floor and get all our paraphernalia around us and the dominoes to play a game or two. Suddenly, something run pass me and I look, and it looks like a little chipmunk and that scared the daylights out of me. I jump up and grab everything and hightailed it to our bedroom to sit on the bed. It is funny now, but not so much then. I am asking Rodney, what is going on? Did you see that? We are sitting looking at each other like, this has never happened before. Look people, I have been getting high for twenty years and never has anything remotely happened like this before. We pull out our Bibles and start reading again.

The next day we are getting high and Rodney has this habit of putting incense everywhere. There is a wall vent toward the floor, and he sticks an incense there and suddenly there is smoke filling the house. It wasn't funny then but as I am sitting here writing, it's making me think how crazy we were. What had happened was, the incense had fallen in the vent hole under the house and so we were scrambling to get rid of all the paraphernalia (pipes, torches, etc…) so we could call the fire department. The firemen came and doused the place where the incense was, but no fire or harm had been done. We were looking all stupid and high as kites. I often wondered if they knew we were high because it sure was evident that we were.

The next move was to grab some clothes and stuff and hit the road. We stopped at the crack house, loaded up with more drugs and off we went. Heading out of town on I-10, we stop at a little motel along the way going toward Tucson. We are in there worrying about, there being too much smoke and someone smelling the crack. So after just a few hours there, we leave. Back on the road again. Stopping along the way to take a hit here and there.

We are being so reckless and acting like mere fools. Eventually we get to Tucson. By the time we get there, Rodney and I are having all kinds of disagreements. We didn't even make it to my Son's house before we were headed back to Yuma, due to the fact that, we are cussing each other out. I get so mad at him that I jump in the back seat still fussing and acting like fools. All of this prompts us to stop at another motel along the way 'cause now we have tired ourselves out. When we get inside, we both have calmed down and he goes to get us something to eat. I get in the shower while he is gone.

While in the shower, I clearly hear a voice say, "You must do this together, you don't get to pick and choose." So when Rodney gets back, I am sitting on the bed and I tell him in a very soft voice, "That we must do this together and that we don't get to pick and choose. The look on his face is as if he has heard this before and he comes over and hugs me intently. We eat and go to bed. In the morning back to Yuma we go.

Our first stop is at the house to get refreshed by showering and change of clothes and back to bingeing again. By now it is the eighth of September. We had been on this binge since the fourth of September. We searched all day for some crack, and it was truly a waiting game. By night fall we had found everything but crack. So we take what we had found (ice), marijuana and some drink and went to a motel right in Yuma. We felt our quest was about to be over because we were just about out of money and it was time to get back to work. But more importantly it seems like a wind down to something more. We are in this motel and we get comfortable and lay out the drugs that we have. Tonight, is not feeling like all the days before. It was an atmosphere of fear. It was like the presence that had been with us, had left. I pull out the Bible and I started reading scripture and Rodney goes and gets in the shower.

He yells to me and says, "Why are you reading so loud?" I told him that I had heard that the word of God would chase the devil away. So I kept reading. When he got out of the shower, he started talking to me and surprisingly he has gone off on some tangent saying, "Why do I let every woman that comes in his life take me away from God?" I looked at him like he was crazy and told him that I was not trying to stand in his way with his relationship with God. He comes around the bed and sits beside me and the next thing I know, his upper body falls back on the bed with his legs hanging off the bed and God lifts his body off the bed three times. I don't even flinch.

He then sits up and ask me "What just happened?"

I said, "God just lifted your body off the bed three times. He looks at me in amazement and stands up in front of me and he is looking at the ceiling as if, he is listening while someone is speaking to him. The next thing that comes out of his mouth was information that he could not have known, unless God had told him because it had just been a thought in my mind. Afraid, I jump off the bed and I go in the bathroom and start repenting and praying. There is no way on God's green earth that Rodney could have known what he had just said to me.

Then he shouts from the other room and say that he just saw an angel stick his head from under the bed and smile at him. I came to look and saw nothing. Just for the record. I believed him because of what he had just told me. Then the Lord spoke to him and told him to get out of the room and go home. You should have seen us scrambling, throwing pipes and cigarettes and dope down the toilet. Alcohol had to go too. Rodney was very adamant that we had to go now. This is the morning of September 9, 2003.

In the car I am asking Rodney, "What does His voice sound like?"

I am excited and curious and nervous all at the same time. Rodney couldn't explain it. All kinds of thoughts went through my head. Like what did we do to deserve a visit from Jesus Christ? Or are we in trouble for the way we cut up for almost a week now. I am thinking, *Wow! No one is going to believe us.* Then the next thought is "It doesn't matter whether they believe or not, I know it happened and Rodney and I are each other's witnesses. We pull into our driveway and get out of the car and into the house we go. Immediately Rodney sits at the kitchen table and starts reading the Bible in the book of Ezekiel. Now, I am back to asking questions again. My first question was, did He, meaning Jesus tell you to start at Ezekiel? And when Rodney didn't answer me, God threw his body down to the ground. I'm standing there, looking like "oops." Then he gets off the floor and back in the chair again.

I then ask Rodney, "What do I suppose to do? Again, God throws him again, this time I heard his head hit the floor. I am really concerned now. My hand is covering my mouth and tears start running down my face. When Rodney gets up this time, I ask him if he is okay and he responds by saying, "He's not going to hurt me Jackie." I am almost relieved. He looks disgusted though. Then I ask him again what do I suppose to do? And he tells me to get on the couch and go to sleep, knowing now that we both have had no sleep for almost a week. So I try to lay down but all of what is going on, I don't want to miss. I go into the kitchen and get a broom and start cleaning the kitchen floor. I walk out of the kitchen and there sitting in our living room is a circle of people (angels, I would suggest, some would say this was a vision) but I say it was more than that, because it was too real.

I ask them, "What if he doesn't fulfill his mission, who will take his place?" No one answered and I then went on to ask everybody what did they want to eat? So I suggested pizza. No one commented so, I left the house and went to Jack-in-the-Box and bought breakfast food.

When I got back and came into the house, Rodney asked me, "Who did you buy all that food for?"

And I looked at him like, "The angels that were here." He looked at me and shook his head. As the day goes on, Rodney is chastised by God all day. He would get tossed to the floor and would not immediately get up and other times he would just get up and have this really ridiculous look on his face. It was like he was getting frustrated but tired all at the same time.

After I eat something, I lay down and fall asleep. When I was sleep, I have a dream. Here is the dream: In the dream, my spirit came out of me and I was looking over a room at a dirty house and a baby sitting there who needed his diaper changed and I began to change him. Then I woke up. Rodney gave me the interpretation of the dream, but I will leave that alone for now. Some things don't need to be revealed.

Later on, in the evening we decided to get some air and take a drive. It had been an amazing day and we still didn't know what it all meant. But we knew that it was going to change our lives forever. While we are cruising after grabbing something to eat, Rodney turns the radio up and then by itself (the radio) goes down. Rodney tells me Jesus is sitting in the back seat. Then he gives me a scripture off the top of his head and I look it up John 14:30. What you must understand here is, that Rodney nor I knew any scripture and there had been a veil over us before and so when he gives me the scripture, it could only have been God. So after that day the throwing around had stopped. As a matter of fact, when we get back home, he didn't get thrown around anymore that day. I call this our "Damascus experience." This was not the last time that God did things to build our faith in Him. "Hear this everybody." Rodney and I never touched another cigarette, alcohol or drug… God took the desire away instantly and we didn't even think about it.

I went back to work and Rodney came to work at my job. We both were selling high speed internet. We were on the same team. I was the top rep and he was catching up to me fast. So there was a contest for the top two performers. The prize was tickets and hotel stay for the Phoenix Suns and LA Lakers and second prize was a TV. Rodney and I won both prizes. Life was getting really good and to top it off, we met a lady with a ministry to the homeless and she invited us to go with her to the mission in Yuma and low and behold one thing led to another and Rodney started preaching.

In December of 2003, Rodney preached his first message at the Crossroads Mission in Yuma, Arizona. Ministry was interesting and exciting. I wanted to go with him every time he preached for support, but he did not want me to after the second time of him ministering to the men. I didn't understand at first but then as I grew in the way of the Lord, I got it. He continued for three years preaching the word at the mission.

After this I couldn't put the Bible down. I couldn't get enough of reading the Bible. I took it to work with me every day. I was determined to know God better, even though I had gone to church as a little girl, the experience was totally different. It was like the eyes of my understanding was open. I read the entire Bible in a couple of months. I started seeing the correlation between the books of the prophets to the book of Revelation. It was awesome!

As time goes on, in this new-found relationship with Jesus Christ, I am asked to speak for Women's Day service. I accept. The preparation was intense because the thought of standing in front of so many people and preaching a message for the first time in my life was horrifying to me. On the day that I was to deliver the message I had indescribable fear. This lady, Renda who had a voice that was so anointed, I had asked her to sing a song (I've Come too far to turn back now) before I was to get up and preach. As she began to sing, the Holy Spirit fell on me and I began to have this indescribable peace, so much so that all fear left me. When she finished singing and I got up it felt like I could conqueror anything. I can't even begin to tell you what it was like. It was so amazing. I couldn't feel my feet on the floor as I walk to the podium. I was thinking to myself if this is what it feels like for the Holy Spirit to take over than, overtake me all the time. It was an amazing time and after this I felt like this is what I should be doing but I didn't pursue it right away. It was stuck in my head that God had called Rodney and not me.

Going to Church now was a must. Life was not right without getting a word on Sunday and Wednesday of every week. It helped me to make it through. I say this because the closer Rodney and I were getting to God, it seemed like the further we were growing apart as a couple.

During this time, his ten-year-old nephew came to live with us. I thought things would get better and Rodney would stop sleeping on the couch, but it never did. We had this facade going on that everything was good, when in fact it was barely, holding on. He had stop preaching at the mission and then…

In November of 2006, I was checking out our bills and looking at our phone bill, when I came across a phone number that should not have been on our call log. To my surprise it was a lady who said that she had been dating Rodney. "You say what!" I am devastated and angry. I told her that she was never to call or talk to my husband again. She was stunned from the sound of her voice. So I suspect that she did not know he was a married man. I ended the conversation with her and jumped in my car and went straight to his job. When I got there, he was just pulling up in his work truck. I looked at him disgusted and angry and I asked him who this woman was (in a very loud voice)! He tells me I was being nosey, and I shouldn't have been looking for nothing!

As a matter of fact, I wasn't looking for anything, I just happened across it. I couldn't believe the words that was coming out of his mouth. If you could have seen the look on my face and my reaction to the way he was acting, like "it's okay that I cheat on you." I can't even begin to express how devastated I was. Looking back on that moment in our life, there had been clear signs, but I missed every last one because of my love for him. I don't know who said "Love is blind," but they were certainly right.

He jumps back in his truck trying to get away from his job so that no one would see us arguing. I get in my car and follow him. I pull up beside him and he speeds off. He avoided me like, "Get away from me and let me do me and you do you." Instead of chasing this joker, I waited for him at home. He kept saying to me that we had not been together in months and so he thought that gave him permission to fool around. "Why do men who cheat on their wives think like that?" I did not talk to him for a long time after this because he didn't make sense and his nonchalant attitude was despicable. My heart hurt real, bad. I thought that, him being a man of God and fearing God, put him in a different place of faithfulness to God and to me. Little by little and day by day the tension in our home began to change. God, for now was making things bearable. I didn't trust him anymore and it put me on the edge all the time concerning his cheating ways. I remember going out and buying a puppy to help ease the unease in our house. I named her "trinity."

In March of 2007 we decided to move to Tucson, Arizona. We both had good jobs we were giving up. Leaving them was not what I thought we should do, but I am going along with what my husband is saying, that this is what God told him. Honestly, I was now lacking faith in anything that he said about God 'cause his actions were not lining up with what was coming out of his mouth.

One thing I have learned in life is everyone can be afforded a second chance. I also thought that a fresh start somewhere else would help us to get back to loving each other again. So we packed up everything and moved to Tucson. Right away Rodney was hired on with a plumbing company and I was still praying for God to give me a better paying job, then the one I just resigned from. I applied everywhere with consistency, with what I did at my old job as supervisor in a call center. I applied at a career college and by the grace of God, I was offered a position and I readily accepted the job because its salary was greater than any salary offered to me before. We secured jobs and the next order of business was to find a house. So one of the Churches in Tucson, had a home that they allowed us to rent for a short time.

By September of 2007 we were moving into a rent-to-own, four-bedroom house with a swimming pool. We sought to buy the house eventually. Again, life was moving right along. Our marriage was not the best. One day out of the blue I checked our phone log again and guess what? Another phone number that should not have been on our call log. I called the number and this woman answered and as I was talking to her, she put him on the phone and when he heard my voice, he dropped the phone. The phone went dead. My next thought was "really." This time around I couldn't understand what was going on with this man that I loved and cherished. My mind can't even comprehend that he is actually having conversations with women on the internet and through text message with me sitting right next to him. He comes home immediately right after getting busted over her house and he tells me that they were just talking.

The nerve of this man to act like I am now just his friend when we are still married and supposed to be in a covenant relationship. I thought we were trying to get our marriage in order, when in fact his heart and mind is a million miles away from me. I can laugh about it now, but it was not funny then. What a fool I had been, especially when I think about this man not being able to hold down one relationship throughout his adult life. But I still loved him.

In December 2007, a few months after moving into this house, and having this last bout with his infidelity, Rodney started acting strange again. We got into a heated argument and the next thing I know he is grabbing his clothes and walking out the front door. All I could think about is, he was waiting for an opportunity to walk out, that's why he started the argument anyway.

Note to men: Just walk; too many times, things are said that cut deep and they may be forgiven but never forgotten.

I cried for days and weeks. Going to work and trying to maintain a smile on my face, because my heart was broken. It had broken, and I did not know if life was worth living anymore. I was now, planning to send his nephew, who now is fourteen back to his grandmother, because Rodney had no intentions of coming home to stay. There are some people who are better off single because that is just how it is. This was Rodney. I didn't want to believe it though. I kept praying for God to bring him home.

In January of 2008, I was standing in my bathroom one morning looking down at a razor blade and thinking, is that going to hurt if I slit my wrist? Will death come immediately so I don't have to feel any more pain? I shook it off and then I thought about the pills in my medicine cabinet, might not be so painful a death, but I shook that thought off too. I rushed out my front door and off to work.

I am sitting in my office and my phone rang and it was the front desk telling me that I had a "walk-in" (a person seeking information about the college courses, no appointment necessary). I went out into the lobby to greet the person and she introduced herself as Mahalia Jackson and I am standing there in shock (not the gospel singer, Mahalia Jackson). Now, for me I immediately see God in this because of what I just went through at home before coming to work.

I escort her back to my office and she and I connect instantly. I tried to get my spiel off about the college courses we offered and immediately it changes to her being an evangelist.

We go deeper into the conversation and I began to tell her of the situation that I had faced standing in my bathroom just moments before. She told me that she had been sent to tell me not to give up and that God is with me. She also said she would be preaching at a church on "A Mountain" (neighborhood that sits at the base of the mountain). I told her that I would be there. We continue to finish up her application for classes. When she left, I couldn't believe that God had cared enough to send a messenger to me, to encourage me. Amazing morning and I was elated. Sunday came and I stepped into this Church, where Mahalia sure enough was about to preach. Before she gets up to preach her daughter gets up to sing and the song is "I've come too far to turn back now," the very song that was sang before I preached for the very first time.

Tears started to run down my face because now the Holy Spirit has come to reassure me that this is God. The more she sang, the greater the peace that came over me. And if that was not enough, Mahalia gets up and her scripture for her message was Isaiah 41:10, "Fear not, for I am with you; Be not dismayed, for I am your God. I will strengthen you, Yes, I will help you, I will uphold you with My righteous right hand."

As she is reading it, the Holy Spirit starts speaking to me in a whisper. "I am with you. I am with you. I am with you." This was so amazing. The message was just what the doctor ordered and afterward, I thanked her for her obedience. The next day I tried calling Mahalia and her phone number did not exist. The information that I had obtained from her was like it never existed. She had just disappeared from the face of the earth (another angel). All I know, from all of this is that God showed up in a mighty way to allow me to know that He cares and not to give up. This helped me a lot with what I was going through because my heart was breaking, and I didn't know if I was coming or going at times. I just want to take a break, to tell God "thank You," for saving me.

The days ahead still seemed so empty without the companionship of my husband, but soon after that my daughter came to live with me from Colorado. She is pregnant and about to deliver her first baby. This was exciting for me because I had not witnessed someone else having a baby. I have had five children of my own and so I knew it would be different, witnessing someone else having a baby. There was so much blood and I thought to myself, how much blood is left in her body? Looked like to me she would certainly need a blood transfusion.

They induced my daughter and my granddaughter was born on April 5 at 5:55 p.m. A week later I had another granddaughter by my oldest son and his wife. Two for two. God always replaces. Arianna and Azariah, for Ivory and Alexandria (my babies that died). Arianna means "most holy," and Azariah means "Yahweh has helped." God is so good. The funny thing about my kids, they purposely did not want me to give their kids biblical names and they ended up giving them biblical names without even knowing. When I told my son. He was amazed. My daughter was like "that's funny." God works in situation even when you think He is not paying attention.

Oh yeah, I forgot to say that Rodney came home for one week after Arianna and Azariah was born as if he was coming back to stay and then he left again. Stupid me. It was a hard lesson to learn.

My Mom and others are telling me that God has something for me, and I insist on it, not being so.

A few months later I get to go to Chicago for an awards dinner because I was the leading representative, to have enrolled the most students at the college I worked at. The accomplishments were also replacing the grief and pain of a marriage gone bad, that I thought was for life.

I preached again at my Church, this time in Tucson for Women's Day. Not by coincidence though. God has a for sure plan, and I am just along for the ride.

In November of 2008 I was at work, sitting in my office and again I get the receptionist telling me I have a walk-in. This time is a gentleman and I usher him back to my office and he sits down and makes me aware that he is a pastor of this little church down the street. So my ears are open to hearing every word that comes out of his mouth. We are conversing and he began to tell me a story of him being over in another country and he is sitting in a doctor's office and someone is talking to him and telling him that God is calling him and as he is saying this, I hear the Holy Spirit say to me "I am calling you." Then the pastor says it again, "God is calling you." I sit silent and pondering on all this. Guess what? This pastor didn't sign up for any classes either. Out the door he goes, and I never hear from him again concerning the classes that he had been so interested in. After work, I am so done because in the past my mom and other people have told me that maybe God is calling me and I would always tell them that "God is not calling me, He is calling Rodney." That couldn't be truer, because Rodney is nowhere to be found. Rodney had also told me that it was me and not him that God was calling.

That evening I decide to take a trip to my mom's in Yuma, Arizona. On my way there, I have plenty of time to meditate on the events of the day. Yuma is a three-and-a-half-hour drive away from Tucson. I get there Wednesday night before Thanksgiving. My mom is excited to see me and I her. We had all the family that lived in Yuma over for dinner. It was an enjoyable time together. Reminded me of the good old days. The highlights are always the leftovers on Friday.

On Saturday about 12:30 p.m. my niece and I are out an about and I decide to stop by Mother Murray's house (one of the church mothers) to see how she is doing. I stop in front of her house and my niece is asking me to take her home because she does not want to wait outside while I shoot the breeze with Mother Murray. As bad as I wanted to tell her to walk on home, I take her, and I decide to try back later.

So I take her home and later that evening I go back to Mother Murray's house. I knock on the door and low and behold Renda, the anointed voice that had sang for me before I preached the first time, opens the door. I am so glad to see her…

Note: Renda, since the first time singing, before I preached, has since moved to California, so why is she in Yuma, Arizona on the same weekend I am? We sit down and I am glad to see Mother

Murray doing good too. Renda started telling me how she was coming around 12:30 p.m. and her husband had told her to wait and go later. Now, understand that this was the original time that I was sitting at Mother Murray's house and didn't go in, because of my niece wanting to go home. So I share this with her, and we are both in awe of God and this now seemly divine meeting is taking place. She goes on to tell me that "God is calling me." Tears are streaming down my face because now in my spirit I sense that God is calling me. The rest of this day is history and I go back to Tucson and I tell my Pastor, Latresa Jester (first African-American woman Pastor of a Baptist Church and now Bishop) that "God is calling me," and she tells me after her ordination as Pastor to the Church, then I can announce my calling before the congregation. So I am going to say on January 18, 2009, I announced my calling to the Ministry of Jesus Christ.

I began my duties under her tutelage. Weeks later I preached my third message, but my first as an upcoming preacher. Two months later I lost my job at the college for no apparent reason. I enrolled more students than any other representative. Go figure.

I could not afford the rent in the four-bedroom house anymore and was forced to move in with my oldest son and his family. It didn't last long and before I knew it, I was going from house to house, to keep from being homeless.

God had placed some good people in my path to make sure that did not happen. So I would like to thank, Maria, Corrina, Elaine, Brian and LaTresa for being there for me.

One day in August of 2009, I was talking with one of my friends (Elaine) and the conversation switched to talking about Rodney. While we are talking, I get a call from his mom. She is telling me that Rodney is trying to call me. He is stranded on the highway on his way to Tucson. Then he calls and tells me the same story but, I find out later that he was never stranded but here in Tucson all along. So I take him back. We have to move from where I am staying because the lady that I am staying with is leery of a man staying in her house. My friend Elaine that I was talking to on the phone when Rodney's mom called is now introducing me to a friend of hers, to put us up for a month because she is about to lose her house. About the time that we are about to be homeless again, my Pastor (Bishop Latresa) and husband, Brian open their home to us. We stay there and Rodney gets a really good job with a well-known plumbing company.

Not long after Rodney started this new job, his same behaviors come up again. This time I am so ready to kick him to the curb because of where I am in God. This was not to be though. He gets fired from this good job. Then he wants to move back to Yuma, and I decide to take him back there, after asking my mom if he can come. She says "yes," and so on the morning of packing his stuff up, he asks me to please come with him and I am reluctant because I have a purpose now and I wanted to see where God is taking me. I prayed and the most I could get out of it was "he is your husband; you have a choice." Well, I chose to go with him and leave behind everything that had been set in motion as far as me becoming a Minister.

No sooner than we get back to Yuma, Rodney gets his job back at the plumbing company that he had left when we lived here before. For me it takes me a minute to find a job. I am still living off my unemployment. I start going back to my old church where I first preached. It was good. Rodney did not attend with me.

I never expected what happened next would affect me, but Rodney's drug habit influenced me right back to doing drugs again after all we had been through. From October 2009 to March 2010 the road was filled with heavy drug use once again. So much so that we racked up a bill we could not afford to pay, and we headed back to Denver in a borrowed car. Six years clean and prospering...

Hard Lessons

Running from a debt you know you can't pay is like looking over your shoulders until time and space happens. "Someday if we happen to meet, I will pay you back. For the borrowed car, I too will repay you."

My life is getting to a place where I am asking myself, "What are you doing?" No answer seems like it is forthcoming. We have moved in with my daughter and granddaughter. Jobs are always the first order of business. How about a month and a half after we get there the drugs start again. My new beginnings are short-lived and getting very old.

Rodney goes behind my back and gets an apartment at the apartment complex that he has gotten a job at. He tells me after the fact and so his name is the only one on the lease.

We move out of my daughter's house into his apartment and it gets really crazy. It's like we have forgotten all the trouble we have escaped by the grace of God.

On this one night we are getting high. I am cooking and smoking. Rodney is smoking, hit after hit. All of a sudden, I see him crawling into the cabinet on the floor next to the stove. His body started shaking and I look closer and he is having a seizure. Then his body goes limp and he stops breathing. He is laying in my arms, and I am crying out to God and reminding God what he said concerning Rodney's life. At that very moment breath comes back into his body and he starts screaming and acting erratically. I tell him what just happens, and he tells me to call an ambulance. I take and flush all the dope down the toilet, and I call the ambulance. They sense that it is drug usage at the hospital, but no one says anything. We get a taxi home and no sooner than we get inside, he wants to call the dope man again.

We both know something must change. Rodney checks himself into a rehab and I am left alone in an apartment that doesn't even have my name on it. I get to stay there three months before I get evicted. Now, before the eviction, I am not totally helpless because I do have a job at the telemarketing place that I had a job, some ten years earlier. I purchase a car from this car dealer down the street from my job. A week later, I get fired for not calling in, but I had.

Back on unemployment, homeless, running around Denver in my newly purchased car, selling dope for other people. I happened over this guy house named Michael, after getting evicted, who I believed to be a good friend with until this one day. I had been driving around and I met this chick who was looking for dope and I took her with me to Michael's house. She winded up getting all cuddly with Michael. I was always on the move, in and out all the time.

One of the times that I had happened back over Michael's house, I was in the bedroom that Michael had given me and this chick had knocked on the door and before I could tell her to come in, she just busted through the door. She made her way over to my bed and sat down and demanded that I give her some crack. I asked her if she had any money and she responded by saying she was waiting on some. I told her I did not have any for sale and she was livid. So I told her to leave. I then had to call out to Michael to get her out of my room. Michael like shunned me as if they had sat in the other room and had decided to bulldog me for my crack.

So I get up and go out into the living room, all the while this chick is on my heels, and all these crackheads are sitting around with no money, begging. When the chick gets tired of begging she decided that she is going to fight me for my dope. We started wrestling at first and then she gets on top of me and I am yelling for Michael to get this chick off me. He did nothing to help me. I scramble really hard and pushed this chick on the floor, off me. I started screaming at Michael and ask him what kind of friend was he. And that I was going to call his girlfriend.

He started yelling back at me and telling me that she can't tell him who he can have in his house. I go in my room and start grabbing my stuff and putting it in my car. I am so hurt that my friend who I have known now for twenty years is taking this chick's side that he barely knows over me. I couldn't understand how this chick had gotten the best of me in a fight because I have never lost a fight. I thought that maybe I was too high, but come to find out she wasn't a chick at all. Just a dude turned into a chick. Then I was really done with Mike 'cause he had to have known this, was a man fighting me if he done messed around with her for a couple of days. Furious, I left and did not go back for quite a while. Eventually I go back to get some of my things I had left on his back porch, but the friendship was never the same again. I was still very fond of Michael because of past experiences with him loaning me large sums of money and providing me a place to lay my head in the many, many years that I had been out here on the streets, but the bond had been broken.

Loyalty on the streets is hard to come by because of the addiction to either the money or the drug. Drug dealers would try to put themselves above the people who smoked it, but they were just as bad as the people they sold too. They treated the smokers bad especially when your money was gone. It was a love, hate relationship. In other words, "I love you when you are spending money with me but when you broke, I hate that you even exist. Now, if you were a smoker and you had a car, then the dope dealer with no car would consider you as a trick. (I know you are wondering why don't the dope dealers, have a car? The dope dealer of today, are not the dope dealer of yesterday. Yesterday dope dealer was much older).

So back to what I was saying; They would wait until you were feening for more dope and they would trick you into loaning your car out to them for a little bit of dope and they would be gone longer than they said. I made that mistake of loaning my car out, but the good part was I knew where my dope dealer lived and eventually, he would have to go home.

November of 2010, the dope dealer that I had been working with and for, had had my car for two days with no communication. He calls me and tells me that he is on his way with my car and that he needs to talk to me. When he gets to where I am, he gives me a dope sack, that he says, "This is his last and should be my last too. When we get into the car, he tells me to drop him off at his house, he begins to tell me that it is all over. That our half-sided partnership is over. He tells me that I don't belong out here and that God has something greater for my life. He says that I am not like all the other people, that I am out here hanging around and that tonight should be my last night too, as it is his last night. Tears are running down my face now because of all that I know about me. I know that God had something greater for me, but I kept getting in my own way.

Now how could this "Crip" be telling me things of God when he is in the world? Note to everybody: God can use anybody. He told me to drop him off at his house and don't ever call him again. You want to know something else, right after I drop him at home, I go home, and my car dies out front of my daughter's house.

We parted ways and if I had totally heeded the message, I would not have gotten busted a month later (December 2010). Number 5 felony and then something in my spirit says, "This is it—this is your last rodeo."

I am watching these cops ride up and down the street, as we are about to pull up to a crack house. I am trying to keep my composure as to not give myself away. There are three of us and two of us get out and go into the house and as we are coming out of the house, the woman that is with me is hounding me for the crack, I just bought.

Now, mind you, she just bought her own, but she is hounding me for mine right in front of these cops. We get into her car and I am warning her to turn around in the seat and drive and keep her eyes on the road. So as we drive off, she is still so concerned with what I got that she can't even drive. Next thing I know the cop is pulling us over and they come to her window and ask for IDs and we all hand them to him. He goes back to his cop car and I am sitting there thinking how am I going to get rid of this dope? I am fussing with the driver because her stupidity just got us busted. Now, mind you, she is not the only one being stupid because I should have gotten out of the car and just walked away but my desire to get high over road everything else that was sensible.

Within seconds he comes back to my side of the car and opens my door and tells me to get out. This man cop is sticking his hands in my pockets and pulls out a crack pipe and a twenty-dollar rock of crack cocaine. Immediately, a whole task force shows up. Busted again and not believing that this is happening to me.

This is the bust that happened on the front page of this book. Busted and disgusted. No understanding how this could have happened and why? Maybe, because I didn't listen to the voice of God, through a young guy a month before. That was my warning and I did not heed it. Shame on me.

By January of 2011 I was sentenced to drug court and failing miserably. I was going to court, high and having dirty urine analysis (UA). The struggle was real. I had just turned fifty years old and I was tired. I didn't have anywhere to live on a regular basis and my life was going down. I was in and out of motels up and down Colfax then…

I hooked (pushing dope) up with a woman drug dealer (Yah). She was the only one who did what she said she would do. (Majority of the drug dealers would make a deal with you and not keep their end of the deal).

I would drive her around and she provided me with a place to stay and food to eat. This was a good (or what I considered good) collaborative partnership until…

We both have a court date coming up but didn't realize that we have the same Judge. We were due in court on the same day. When we go inside the court building, I am asking her what courtroom is she going in? And she said the same one I was going into. We are sitting in courtroom and Yah have to go to the bathroom. When she comes back in the courtroom, they called her name. She went up to the podium and the judge immediately started questioning her and told her that she had a dirty UA. I am stunned and shocked because she does not smoke crack or anything else. The next question blows my mind. The judge asked her if she is pregnant and she says "yes." How could this judge had known that she was pregnant? Now Yah had just informed me that she was pregnant that morning.

The judge waves to the deputy to take her into custody and I am stunned because this was my judge too and never had I ever gotten consequences like this after all the crazy things I had been doing. But I guess we will take in a count that she is pregnant with a dirty UA. The only way she could have gotten a dirty UA would be from the crack cocaine soaking into her pores through the plastic bag. Crack was that serious. Most drug dealers would use gloves to distribute it. I was left holding her personal belongings and watching them take her away. She was in tears. Then the judge called me up.

She ran a couple of questions by me and allowed me to go. I left with my head hung low. Yah is gone and now all I can do is think about her crazy boyfriend that I have to go meet up with to give her personal belongings to and the car that she had purchased for me to drive around. Tears are streaming down my face. "What am I going to do now, where will I stay? There was only one night left on the hotel we had been at. Her boyfriend wasn't as nice as her, and as a matter of fact he was a spiteful cuss. He didn't even treat Yah good.

It was like God was closing one door after another, so that I was left to call on Him. I did and my prayer was "Lord I can't do this anymore. I don't have the power to quit on my own and I need you now to take the desire away once and for all. Amen." Three days after the prayer my daughter calls me and says, "Mom please come home. I need you and you need me." So I go to my daughter's house. I started doing better, slipping every now and again but for the most part, I was determined to get clean once and for all.

My daughter lived two blocks from Colfax and so I was still in the immediate area of all the drug activity. Thank God, though, that one monkey don't stop the show because although Colfax was two blocks away, Montview was two blocks away in the opposite direction and that was my alternative route to Church. So I did my best to avoid Colfax at all cost until I got stronger. Catching the bus downtown to make all my treatment and court dates took added strength but I made it because of the grace of God. Going to Church on a regular basis changed everything for me. The word of God once again was getting down on the inside of me and it got to a place where it was more important to me to get that word instead of being idled minded for outside forces to take control again. Another thing about getting closer to God, it will provoke those outside forces to draw you back by other people actions and intentions.

I was in this treatment program and my case manager received my UA and said that it was dirty, and I told her that she had made a mistake. She had formerly been a parole officer and so when she seen my tears she told me to stop it and that it was her duty to report me to social services, due to the fact that I lived with my daughter and I was a danger to my granddaughter. I poured my heart out to this hard nose woman and she would not listen and check her paperwork again. So I called my Probation officer and she told me that I did not have a dirty UA. I was elated but it was too late to stop the case manager and she told social services.

So they threaten to make me move out of my daughter's house, away from my granddaughter if a dirty UA came up again. That, to me was the final straw or the one that broke the camel's back. I got clean after this. I requested a new case manager and I hated the other one for a long time, because she was so hard that she wouldn't even check to see if she had made a mistake. My Probation officer cleared it all up with her and the courts. It seemed to me that there was one battle after another. Getting clean was not easy.

Right after this battle, God laid it on my heart to write this book. I started writing as to put bits and pieces of my life in the book and giving people advice in my writings. I am pondering on what the title should be. I am lying in bed one morning, half asleep and conscience enough to hear a voice tell me to "rise up." The voice was so clear. Then I knew that was God whispering the title of the book, "Rise Up." I was so excited. It became so clear to me why the title was so fitting. I had gone through so much that, I kept getting back up, but there was another kind of getting up that I would later grab a hold of.

Rodney shows up again in August of 2011 and my daughter would not let him stay in her house, because of the negative influence he had on me. She would in no way, give in.

I went to ask my mom's friend, Juan'el if we could move in with her. She said "yes" and thirty days later Rodney was gone again. I was glad for the chain of events this time because my mom's friend's house was cool, and I liked where she lived. It was away from Colfax and all the drug activity. As for Rodney, I knew that this was our last rodeo because I had come to a place and time in my life that I was not willing to sacrifice my life anymore for drugs or a man. I had this man on a pedestal that should not have ever been, but when you are starving for affection and companionship it will often make you act like a fool.

Since April of 2011 I had been going to church and getting my feet settled once and for all. I got involved a little bit at Church and then I pursued my calling again. In November of 2011 I had all but stopped smoking cigarettes. I prayed and asked God, how was I going to be able to ever get over these cigarettes, if Juan'el (roommate) is still puffing on them every day.

Three days later, Juan'el stops smoking cigarettes. Never in my wildest dreams could this be possible, but it happened. In December of 2011, I stop buying packs of cigarettes and I bought a fake cigarette and puffed on it for a couple of weeks. On December 29, 2011, I get a phone call from one of the upcoming ministers (Divine was her name) that would be starting ministry prep with me on January 3, 2012, she says "God is going to use you and He says whatever you are doing, you should stop it now." When I got off the phone with her because this woman did not even know me, I stopped smoking cigarettes that day, 12/29/2011. So glad I listened.

I start Ministry Prep class and it is going good. One of the ministers (Laverne) invites me to a Bible Study that she leads, and I accept. Around about the third time going to this Sunday night bible study, the leader had not gotten there yet and we are sitting around the table about five to six people and I was sharing some of what I had been through. The minister who was playing on the guitar stopped in mid-stream and looked at me and started speaking in tongues. Now, I had never known this person until attending this Bible study, and I still did not know him. I was introduced to him, so I knew his name to be Minister Steven. So as he is speaking in tongues, in my head I am telling Jesus Christ that he is speaking in tongues and I don't understand a word he is saying. Then he stops and this is what he said: You are a Prophet of the Most-High God.

God has given you the spirit of Elijah, with a double portion and the gift of healing. I see two doves flying over your head right now and they are about to enter you right now and that was the interpretation of the tongues," he says. He also said to me "I was instructed to tell you last week, but I could not minister to you because my wife was not here." I look around to see who his wife is, and she is sitting right beside me. She has only one arm and I smile at her; all the time tears are streaming down my face. This day is January 29, 2012. I am thinking to myself, *What in the world?* This message is so resonating in my spirit. I can't stop thinking and mediating on this. The very next week I come back to the Bible study again and afterward we are putting up the chairs and I see this woman coming toward me and she begin to talk and tell me "God says your prayers are powerful and they are shaking the gates of hell."

I look at her and I ask her, "Where did you come from?"

She said I was standing over by the door and God pointed you out and told me to come tell you that. She turns and walks away. I don't know what to say or what to think at this point. Last week one message and the next week another, and both are shaking me to my core. I think it is also appropriate to tell you both people who gave me the two messages were not African American.

I thought this was all falling (the call of God), to Rodney and maybe now, God has chosen me is all I can think. (Note to self: Remember when I said to the angels sitting in my living room that day "if Rodney does not complete the mission, who would take his place? I did not know why then; did I ask that question). But to do what? I am pretty excited, and I tell a few people and they are not as excited. So I try to keep it to myself and see what God will do.

I get a call one day while working on my book, and it is a lady from a local television station, and they are asking me to go on the TV show to talk about Drug Court and how it helped me. You know I did not turn that down. I am so amazed at the things that are happening in my life. This is another one of my "God moments."

After graduating from Drug Court in May of 2012, I continued to give back by mentoring to those who were and are currently in drug court. Five years strong and I am still one of the leaders of that group.

What is important about this moment in my life is, I had been in the court system for two years and now I am free and very cautious of any entertaining spirits toward drugs. I had to get to a place where it's done, once and for all. Too much at risk and I was not willing to put my life on the line for anybody ever again. All pedestals that I had put certain people on had all been destroyed. Now, I could start living my life on God's terms.

It was a couple months after finishing drug court that my mom came to town. I am always excited when my mom comes to town. We are barbecuing over my younger sister's house because it is the Fourth of July. On the way over, Juan'el and I are driving over to her house and we get to the corner of Sixth/Sable at a red light and I am driving Juan'el's car. This man pulls up beside us. He says, "Ms. Lady, Ms. Lady" (he is looking around Juan'el to get eye contact with me), "you are a great woman of God." The Lord is your Shepherd and in 2012 God is going to tell you well done." The light turns green and he drives off.

Juan'el looks at me and she says, "Do you know him?" and I say, "I have never seen that man in my life." When we get to my sister's house, Juan'el tells my mom, "If I had not seen and heard it for myself, I would have never believed it." My mom is surprised by these words. It seems to me that God is keeping me encouraged and growing my faith for what's ahead. How could this man, who I had never seen before, know that I quoted the Twenty-Third Psalms daily: The Lord is my Shepherd. The "God moments" are coming in times to remind me to keep pressing on.

That same month (July 2012) I, along with about thirty others get ordained to be Elders (ministers) at The Potter's House Church of Denver. This was another highlight in my life. And if the devil wasn't already mad because of me stepping into my calling, I get news that I have a spot on my breast in August of 2012. All kinds of thoughts are running through my head. "Lord I thought you told me that I would do great things and now I have a spot on my breast?"

So I go into the ultrasound and biopsy on the same day. Then they want me back for an MRI. The results are forthcoming. The elders (ministers) and deacons have been invited to a meeting with Prophet Ruckins McKinley. On the day, that he comes is the same day I get my test results back. The results are, it is cancerous. Later, that evening, I go to the church and the meeting is taking place in the chapel. I am in tears because of the news I just got. One of the elders walk up to me who was on staff, and she says, "no worries, the prophet already spoke about you." I am perplexed and as soon as she walks away a Pastor walks over to me and say "no worries the prophet already spoke about you. Imagine, they use the same words, literally.

What I have learned is that earlier that same day, the staff had met with the prophet and he prophesy that there was someone among them with a spot and that is just how the doctor described it to me. The meeting that evening started, and the Prophet spoke into a lot of the people's lives, but he never got around to me. The benediction is done, and I immediately walk up to the Pastor and asked him what about me and he said, "no worries," and he calls over the Prophet and he says, "God wants you to know two things. One, your fear will give it power and two, David walked through the valley of the shadow of death, it is not death, it is just a shadow and when you wake up in the morning, you say "it's just a shadow" and when you go to bed at night you tell it, "it is just a shadow." Then he prayed over me. I did as I was instructed every day and night. In October, the doctor removed it and she said it was a perfect little round ball. The doctors wanted me to do radiation. I opted not to do the radiation. When you get a word from the Lord it will change your mind concerning what other people think you should do. I took the pill, generic of Arimindex. Breast cancer free. Thank you, Jesus!

After catching my breath from the trial of the cancer, I settle into my duties at the Church. I begin by writing letters for the Prison ministry, I served in the Children's ministry, Bereavement, New Beginnings, Altar and Baptism ministries. I am so in my zone now, loving life and loving, giving back.

The night of October 31, 2013, I got a phone call that my grandma has passed away. Catherine Hampton lived to see 102 years.

Her Birthday had just passed on September 26. My sisters and I prepared to go to Virginia for her funeral. I was asked to do the prayer of solace at the funeral.

While there, I was able to see my dad. We didn't have much to talk about, but it was good to see him never-the-less. It was good to see a lot of family members that I had not seen in over forty years.

After staying in Juan'el's condo for three and a half years, it was time to move on. Shout out to you Juan'el, thank you. A friend offered me a room in her house, and another good friend payed my rent for three months.

In January of 2016, I was sitting with my youngest Son, Caster watching the NFL playoffs at his house. Out of the blue I ask my son, "Son what is Uber?" He told me and three days later I signed up and started driving. (Only because the Church had allowed me to be the recipient of a donation of a car donated to the Church for someone in need. I was so grateful that I was chosen).

I was addicted immediately to driving because now I am making my own money and paying my rent myself. It was a fulfilling experience. Not having to beg and borrow from anybody any longer was great. I would like to say though that God will open doors, to have you taken care of but to human understanding it's still looks like begging and borrowing. The struggle had been real but not without tears of joy. God kept "Wowing! me through the entire process of me getting on my feet.

About a month after I started driving, the announcement came that a second trip to Israel was underway, (see I was not financially able to go on the first trip).

I thought I can drive enough to afford this trip and I was determined to take the trip of a lifetime to Israel. Never in all my life would I have imagined a trip to Israel with no money saved and no bank account at all. This was a great turning point for me. I soon got a bank account and then I drove day and night to make sure I was on that plane when the time came. God was making a way even though I couldn't see it. People were tipping me with grand tips and the rides were turning into a ministry. I shared my story of my trials and successes, and they were so inspired. I can't even begin to tell you how gratifying this all was. Ministry outside of the four walls of the Church, I loved it. Coming down to the final days before the trip was so exciting. Many people had told me how life changing the experience to Israel would be. I could hardly wait to experience it for myself. I had never been out of the country except the borders of Mexico and Canada. This time I had to have a passport and for the first time in my life, I was feeling all grown up.

The day came, November 1, 2016. I was so excited, that the long flight was not a factor. Flying over oceans though was not appealing to me. But here we go. Our journey started from Denver to New York and then to Tel Aviv. What was interesting to me was that we were going to see almost all of Israel. We stayed in three different hotels in three different parts of the country. First, Netanya by the Mediterranean Sea, for one night. Then on to the Sea of Galilee for two days. So much information from the tour guide and everything still feeling like just a normal trip. We are leaving the Sea of Galilee and we stop by the clear part of the Jordan River and we get baptized. That was amazing. I saw fish actually swimming in the river. It was so cool. We all took plenty of pictures of everything. On the way to Jerusalem we stopped at the part of the Jordan where it is believed that Jesus Christ got baptized. The water was very muddy. There we did a foot washing and that was cool. Other people saw our leaders performing this ceremonial task and they too wanted their feet washed as well. It was amazing.

Next stop was Jerusalem. When the bus was on the outskirts of the great city and you can see this city sitting high, there are no words to describe it. I thought to myself, the movies I had seen, had done it justice. It was so amazing! Right out of a picture book. As we glazed upon it the tour guide started playing the song, "Jerusalem." We saw shepherds with their tents and sheep and goats on the side of the highways. It was so surreal. Before settling into our hotel, we went over to Bethlehem. I was excited but after getting over there the presence of the soldiers took away from the experience because a few were very rude and disgruntled. The Nativity place was just okay because of the long wait to get to see it. By the time I got to see it, I was exhausted. We took group pictures and that was exciting. Our group was approximately eighty-five people. We supported a lot of the local shops and there was this one guy who followed us everywhere trying to get us to buy scarfs and such. He was pretty cool. While being over in Bethlehem one of the men saw one of the young ladies that were a part of our group and offered to buy her for a few livestock.

That too was interesting. She is beautiful but, "no thank you" was our answer. So back to Jerusalem to get something to eat and rest before journeying through this great city. On this night, I prayed, and my prayer was "God, I have been here three days and no life changing moment has happened yet, amen." That next day I was expecting great things. We started at the top of the Mount of Olives and down into the Garden of Gethsemane and that was where the expecting started. Being there in the garden, I felt the very presence of the Lord. So much so that tears started running down my face. I knelt down at the rock that Jesus Christ supposed to have knelt to pray before being arrested. It was a moment I will never forget.

Then we traveled on to the entrance (sheep gate) of the old city of Jerusalem with the wall around it. As we are walking in there, there is this church and it is where Mary's mother's house is. Now, just to educate you, they built a church over almost every significant historical house or place, so they would be protected and preserved. We are walking pass it and we come to the Pool of Bethesda. Before taking pictures, the tour guide asked us to sit in this seated area so that he can give us some background history on the area. As he is speaking the Holy Spirit tells me to look up and I look up and flying overhead is a pure white dove and immediately I point and tell the group to "look!" and everyone looked up to see the dove too and they are amazed as well. After he finish talking, we get up and I turn around and look up and there are two white doves sitting on the roof top. Amazing sight to see. So I ask the tour guide if this was a normal sighting and he responded by saying, "In all of my forty years I have never seen that before." I took a little video of them sitting on the roof and pondered on what this could mean. Footnote: a white dove is a sign of the Holy Spirit presence in some cases.

I believe God set that up just for us. We tour the rest of the city and I am still pretty stoked over the doves that everything else just seemed more amazing as well. Walking down the Via Dolorosa and knowing that some of the stones were actual dated back to Jesus Christ time, was pretty exciting. I am feeling like I am walking on a cloud and not wanting to come down. It was truly a life changing day. Watch what you pray for, you just might get it. I am so glad I prayed.

We ventured to the skull of Golgotha and there we took Holy Communion. When we finished up, we proceeded just a few feet away to the actual tomb where Jesus Christ was laid after His crucifixion. It was a beautiful garden. There were almond trees with some still remaining almonds on them. I took a picture of it. Later that night back at the hotel, in my room I looked at the pictures and low and behold there was my third white dove flying over the almond tree from the visit to the tomb. This was a good day.

In the final days, we toured Masada and visited the Dead Sea. I floated in the Dead Sea. I can say I did it, and I never have to do that again. I didn't like the way it made my hands feel. It was like silk and I couldn't get it off, until I showered. What an experience that was.

The last day there we went to Museums such as the holocaust. That was not fun, but a sad time. To see pictures of all the lives lost. The graves, that were not graves at all but a travesty of man's inability to treat another human as if it was his own life. I walked out feeling lost. That part of the tour should happen somewhere in the middle. It will leave a lasting impression of what this nation suffered at the hands of a deranged tyrant.

Israel was all that it was meant to be and more. I wouldn't have wanted to miss it for anything. When I read my Bible now, it's more real because I was standing in the place that it happened, for the most part.

This life has been an amazing journey, whether it was good or bad. Sometimes self-inflicted and other times, life just happened. Many times, I should have thrown in the towel, but I was not built like that. I did not know I had an option to quit. But all in all it has been a divine journey, one that I am glad I didn't miss.

Let me share the revelation that I have been given: "to get up" is a physical action, but "to Rise Up" is a spiritual action. I pray that this will resonate in your very soul so whatever needs to change in your life, will. When you finally find out, that you are not doing life just because and you are actually doing life on purpose, a whole new world opens up to you. Many times, I tell the addiction group that I facilitate, when you know that you have a purpose for being here, that is where I began to live. That's where I began to live. Before it was mere survival, so I thought, but in a sense… It was survival until I collided with my purpose. I want to see what the end is going to be.

As I come to a pause in my story, in March of 2017, I was sitting on my bed putting on my pajama shirt on, I felt a golf ball size lump under my left breast. First thought was "Not again." I wanted to believe anything but cancer. Sure, enough the doctor said, "This time it is bigger and more aggressive, and chemo and radiation will definitely be needed." I was not willing to hear the voice of doom when I knew that my God was bigger than that. Surgery happened, all margins were clear, and I chose not to do chemo nor radiation. Trusting God on this one too! Today I am cancer free. Thank you, Jesus!

Three months later, the news that I had not want to come came. My stepmom called and she said "your dad is not doing well and the doctors said that he doesn't have many days left. She went on to say that she would hold the phone to his ear so that I could talk to him. I told my dad that I loved him with tears streaming down my face. I told him that in spite of not spending more time with him, I loved him so much.

Three days later, the news came that my dad had died. My sisters and I prepared to drive to Virginia to lay my dad to rest.

My only disappointment was my dad not being able to see the woman that God handpicked and designed for such a great future. He always wanted a boy to be proud of, but I wanted him to know that daughters can be just as wonderful as sons.

"Rest in heaven, Dad, you gave me lessons that no one else could give. Through the bad and good times, I learned valuable nuggets to get through this life. I will always love you."

This closes the chapters of great hardship for me. Not that there will not be any greater challenges but I get to walk with Jesus Christ now. He is the light in my life and when I walk with Him there is no darkness. I believe that my greater is on the way and I am excited. This is not the end but the beginning of miracle, signs, and wonders.

I thought this year would end pretty smooth but another test has to take place. Rodney starts his crap again but this was all in God's plan and I pass the test this time and when I had made a decision never to touch drugs again. January comes in with a bang. Rodney wakes up on the second of January and tells me he gotta go. I am like, "What are you talking about?"

He said, "I am finally going back to North Carolina."

Then, the next thing shocks me even more when he says, "I have given my two week notice to the apartment complex. Listen, he is the maintenance supervisor for this complex and if he is gone, I have to go too, because the rent would not be affordable for me alone."

I am standing with my mouth wide open like, "What the world is happening?" I don't press him because I know this is God, removing him from my life.

Now I have to take him serious because if I don't I am going to be left in the cold. This is not the first time Rodney has done a disappearing act on me and so why should this time be any different. But it is different, because he has never ever said he is going back to the east coast.

Reality is slapping me in the face for the first time in my life 'cause I have never lived by myself before. After securing me a nice apartment with all the bells and whistles, on move in day, Rodney helps me move in and he has his truck pack to the hilt, ready to head back to his Mom's in North Carolina.

I move in on January 20, 2018. Rodney leaves on the twenty-first and I lose my job with Uber on January 22, 2018. Totally devasted after a few days, because I can't imagine this is happening, but I am trying to keep my faith that God has got me. By April 30, 2018, I have had to get a nine-to-five to pay the bills. By September I have gotten three eviction notices on my door for the past three months. I managed to come up with the rent and all the late fees until October. I got tired of that headache and worrying every single month and so I decided it was time to find a place more affordable. Trying to find that in Denver or Aurora was not going to be easy but my hope was in Jesus Christ and I knew that He had a plan. Well, I talk to one of the pastors at my Church and low and behold he had a place for rent and so I moved in there after contemplating it for two weeks. Right after I move in, I began to have horrible stomach pains and so I went to the hospital. They ran test and when the test came back the doctor told me to go to the emergency room right away. Come to find out, I was going to need surgery to remove part of my intestine 'cause there was an infection. They attribute it to eating pork that was not done. Guess what, I remember the day that I had the pork at a restaurant, and I thought to myself that, that's not done enough but I ate it anyway. After surgery, I am out of work for six weeks healing.

One trial after another, and I am like saying to God, "Have I not been tested enough? Have I not trusted You?" Knowing that God has promised me a great future, I realize that giving up is not an option. I have to press on and stay focus.

My story has taken me over nine years to write, from the first time God told me too. I understand now why. This is the perfect time to *rise up*. So much is going on in the world and everyone is going to need to hope in someone or something but that will not be good enough. Our hope must be in the One who can move heaven and hell, in a blink of an eye, and I am here to tell you, that, that is why I am still standing because my hope has been in Jesus Christ.

Don't give up; rise up.

About the Author

Jacqueline, also known as Jackie, grew up in a little town called "Hampton" to Joseph and Barbara Hampton. After completing one year at Hampton High School, her mother left her abusive dad and moved her daughters to Tucson, Arizona. In her final year of high school, she got pregnant but still went on to graduate from Tucson High School. College was not in her immediate future. At twenty-two she became addicted to crack cocaine. Marriage happened and four more children, but after losing two children to SIDS, the journey became unbearable. Jackie took to the streets of Denver and Aurora where death was staring her in the face and prison was inevitable with the path she was on. She could not escape the trials and tribulations, but all the while, she knew someone was watching out for her. Destined, chosen, and anointed.

CPSIA information can be obtained
at www.ICGtesting.com
Printed in the USA
JSHW031335280821
18222JS00001B/1

9 781098 083403